SYMBOLS AND MEANING

SYMBOLS AND MEANING

A Concise Introduction

MARI WOMACK

A Division of
ROWMAN & LITTLEFIELD PUBLISHERS, INC.
Walnut Creek • Lanham • New York • Toronto • Oxford

ALTAMIRA PRESS
A division of Rowman & Littlefield Publishers, Inc.
1630 North Main Street, #367
Walnut Creek, CA 94596
www.altamirapress.com

Rowman & Littlefield Publishers, Inc.
A wholly owned subsidary of The Rowman & Littlefield Publishing Group, Inc.
4501 Forbes Boulevard, Suite 200
Lanham, MD 20706

PO Box 317
Oxford
OX2 9RU, UK

British Library Cataloging in Publication Information Available

Library of Congress Cataloging-in-Publication Data

Womack, Mari.
   Symbols and meaning : a concise introduction / Mari Womack.
      p. cm.
   Includes bibliographical references and index.
   ISBN 13: 978-0-759-10322-1

1. Symbolic anthropology. 2. Signs and symbols. 3. Symbolism. I. Title.
   GN452.5.W66 2005
   306.4—dc22

                                                           2004022282

Printed in the United States of America

To Jacques Maquet, who has guided me in my study of symbols and expressive culture, to Arnold van Gennep, my intellectual and biological ancestor, and to Alfred van Gennip, who never had a chance to express his genius. I love you. May you live forever in our hearts and minds, as you live forever in my heart.

CONTENTS

PREFACE

When I transferred from the Department of Psychology to the Department of Anthropology as an undergraduate at UCLA, little did I know that I would stumble into a "Forest of Symbols" (Turner 1967). I had been headed for a specialization in physiological psychology and had little interest in speculation about the vagaries of the human mind. As I say later in this book, the mind will not show up on an autopsy.

But scholarly research has a way of leading us down previously unexplored paths. Much to my surprise (and occasional horror), I found myself becoming enraptured by the exotic flora and fauna symbols evoke. To study symbols is to study the most profound of human experiences. I count myself blessed.

Among my intellectual ancestors is Arnold van Gennep, author of *Les rites de passage*, a classic text on the ritual aspects of symbols. Not only is he my intellectual ancestor, he is also my biological ancestor, or at least he figures prominently on my lineage. In the mid–nineteenth century, my biological ancestor emigrated from Europe to become the founding father of all the Van Gennips in the United States. His fifteen-year-old brother, Alfred van Gennip, was killed by border raiders during the Civil War. Robert, the younger brother, protested, and the border raiders threatened to kill him too. I cry today because that younger brother had the courage to hide his tears. But I also exist because of his unshed tears.

Imagine my astonishment when studying anthropology in the UCLA Department of Anthropology to discover that Arnold van Gennep had founded an entire school of study that included research on ritual and symbolism. There could be no mistake. The Dutch designation "van" has the same meaning as the German designation "von" and the French designation "de." It means "of the place of." During World War II, my aviator uncle flew over the lands of "Gennep." Based on navigation maps, he reported that Gennep lands had been flooded during the war. If there are "Gennep" survivors in Europe, I would be happy to hear from them. I would want them to know that the American branch of the family is carrying on the tradition that Arnold van Gennep established so long ago.

But there are other ancestors who are intellectual rather than biological. Jacques Maquet shares two of my consuming interests: symbolic anthropology and expressive culture. As I was breaking new ground by studying rituals of professional athletes, Jacques was writing his book *The Aesthetic Experience: An Anthropologist Looks at the Visual Arts* (Yale University Press, 1986). Jacques has the rare ability to conceptualize broadly and think coherently. His advice allowed me to frame the apparently unruly realm of athletes and symbols in coherent terms (Womack 1982).

To Jacques Maquet and Arnold van Gennep, as well as Alfred van Gennip, I humbly dedicate this book.

I have never met anyone who knows more about symbols than Douglass Price-Williams. When I would come up with a "new" idea, Douglass would reply, "Check out page 215, Jung's *Collected Works*, volume 5" or "Look up Rodney Needham." Douglass reminded me of something that all good artists and writers know: "All creative effort arises out of recombining what has gone before." Douglass made me realize that everything I could imagine had been said before. In some cases, I learned, my intellectual forebears had said it better.

This heady venture into the world of symbols led me to long for my "logical-positivist" roots. For this enhancement of my intellectual growth, I turned to Allen Johnson, noted for his emphasis on empiricism. Here I found a kindred soul. When I asked him to chair my dissertation committee and noted that I would be studying rituals of professional athletes, he replied, "Compile a hundred-item bibliography of books and articles relating to the topic." I returned, some months later, bearing what I considered the definitive bibliography on symbols and the psychology of athletic competition. I proudly tendered the manuscript. Without accepting the manuscript, Allen said, "Now cut it down to thirty." I learned another important lesson. A scholar does not truly know her field until she learns to "cut it down to thirty." This remains my motto. But there is another important principle at work here. Allen did not claim title to my research. Instead, he demanded that I claim agency over my own work.

The physicist Richard Feynman advocated the idea that a good teacher can help even an uninterested student learn complex concepts by using simple examples and relating them to students' experience. When he tried to teach an artist friend about electricity and magnetism, the friend was more interested in finding out how to fix his car. Feynman writes, "When I tried to show him how an electromagnet works by making a little coil of wire and hanging a nail on a piece of string, I put the voltage on, the nail swung into the coil, and Jerry said, 'Ooh! It's just like f----g!'"[1] I have called on Feynman's teaching philosophy in writing this book. Scholars can extrapolate from this simple exposition. Those who are just beginning to enter the "forest of symbols" can chart their way with this guide book.

I dedicated my book *Sport as Symbol: Images of the Athlete in Art, Literature and Song* (McFarland 2003) to Victor Turner, who first recognized the importance of my study of professional athletes. He also figures prominently in this volume. He and Susanne Langer virtually defined symbols as we study them today. Though symbols arise out of the unconscious, they are shaped by the social context. As Chinese philosophers have long noted, individuals and societies are not antithetical; one cannot exist without the other.

At the same time, scholars cannot exist without their families. I never got to meet Arnold van Gennep or Alfred van Gennip, but they are no more esteemed than the family in which I grew up. Our dinner table conversation was dominated by political and philosophical debates. Reading was an avocation shared by all. Sometimes we went without what some considered the "necessities" of life—new shoes, a warm winter coat—but we were never so poor that we could not afford two daily newspapers.

Today, my most esteemed colleagues are my children: Jeff, Greg, and Laura Womack. Whenever I am in doubt on a personal or intellectual issue, I turn to them. Because they love me and know my history, I always get good advice, guided by love and undiluted by hopes of personal gain. Their advice is often guided by their own partners and councilors, Michelle Gravatt Womack and Richard Williams.

I also get good advice—and a great example—from my neighbors Herb and Julie Hill. Herb is an internationally renowned ornithologist from whom I learned to distinguish an egret from a seagull. Julie is a respected artist who has recorded "what no longer exists," the buildings and environs of San Pedro that have disappeared in the development of an international seaport.

Nancy Roberts of Prentice Hall knows academic publishing like no other. She advised me to take this book to Mitch Allen of AltaMira Press because of her high regard for him. As always, she was right. I have worked with Rosalie Robertson, a warm and caring editor who nurtures the souls of anthropologists. Perhaps more importantly, her pace equals mine. Kristina Razmara and Jason Proetorius escorted *Symbols and Meaning* safely across the finish line.

To these acknowledgments, I must add others. I would not have written this book had Tom Curtin not suggested it. Alice Kehoe and Claire Farrar made comments that helped to shape the book's final form. Dr. H. B. Kimberley Cook was an inspirational guide through my exploration of my own Forest of Symbols. Karen Eileen Saenz, while undergoing her own turbulent journey through the Forest of Symbols, contributed greatly to my exploration of my unconscious. In addition, I owe a great deal to Karen's editorial advice that I end the book with the symbolic journey of Heaven's Gate cult members into outer space. Their journey into unexplored territories on the physical plane enhanced my understanding of exploration of territories on the inner, unconscious plane. Not all journeys can be framed in an empirical universe.

I have illustrated some points in *Symbols and Meaning* with examples from my anthropology classes. In all cases, I have altered the circumstances so they accurately portray the gist of the exchanges without impinging on the privacy of the individuals involved.

The book contains some repetition, especially in the case of citations. I sought at first to eliminate repetition. After long consideration, I decided to retain the repetitions as an aid to fellow scholars—who are always searching for ethnographic examples—and to illustrate the multiple applications of symbols.

No mere human could write the definitive essay on symbols, and I have not presumed to do so. To all those, seen and unseen, living and ancestral, who created an environment in which this book could be written, I offer thanks.

NOTE

1. From Richard P. Feynman, *"Surely You're Joking, Mr. Feynman!": Adventures of a Curious Character*, ed. Edward Hutchings (New York: Norton, 1985), 262.

1

UNDERSTANDING SYMBOLS

"Tonight, in this very city, someone will die for a symbol." I often make this statement in my cultural anthropology classes to startle my students, gain their attention, and drive home the point that there is no such thing as "just a symbol." I can make this statement with confidence since I teach in Los Angeles, a city with multiple levels of gang culture, often-violent subcultures that rely on symbols to establish identity and enforce conformity within the group. However, the same assertion could be made about New York City, Buenos Aires, Kabul, Sarajevo, Moscow, Cairo, Baghdad, Hong Kong, Bangkok, or Lagos.

No one can escape the power of symbols. If we are not involved in the symbolic complexes of religion and magic, we observe symbolic dramas on television, at the movies, or on the sporting field. If we manage to evade the influence of symbols in our daily lives—which is virtually impossible—we will still encounter symbols in our dreams. Wherever we look, our world is "peopled" with gods, heroes, and demons[1] who act out our hopes, fears, conflicts, and triumphs on the large screen of mass media or on the small screen of our dreams. Symbols are the language of religion, magic, and expressive culture, including art, literature, theater, music, festivals, and sporting events.

SYMBOLS AND COMMUNICATION

Symbols are, above all, a means of communication. In general terms, symbols are images, words, or behaviors that have multiple levels of meaning. Symbols stand for concepts that are too complex to be stated directly in words. Based on his work among the Ndembu of northwestern Zambia, in Africa, Victor Turner notes, "One aspect of the process of ritual symbolization among the Ndembu is . . . to make visible, audible, and tangible beliefs, ideas, values, sentiments, and psychological dispositions that cannot directly be perceived" (1967, 50). The social anthropologist Raymond Firth writes, "It is assumed that symbols communicate meanings at levels of reality not accessible through immediate experience or conceptual thought. . . . These meanings are often complex and of different layers" (1973, 49).

If I say "Let's have lunch," I am referring to the specific act of ingesting nutrition. This act may also involve social rewards since I am choosing to consume nutrients with someone whose company I enjoy or whose aid I wish to solicit. If I pay for lunch, I am conveying additional meanings, which may include subtle bribery for the aid I am seeking or enhancement of my own social status through the demonstration of my power to pay. Seeking favors and negotiating social status are such common aspects of social life that we typically fail to take note of them. Their meaning is implicit.

When we have recourse to symbols, the subtleties of communication increase exponentially. Food itself may take on symbolic properties. If I take communion in the Roman Catholic Church, for example, I am participating in an act that is both social and spiritual. As defined by the Catholic Church, the communion is with God as expressed in the relationship of human beings to Jesus Christ. The communion both represents the body of Christ and, in Catholic belief, *is* the body of Christ. At the same time, the *communion* ritual is *communal*. I am demonstrating my membership in a *community* of believers. Similarly, if I am Jewish and partake in the Friday night Shabat, I am communicating multiple levels of involvement: in my relationship to G-d, in Jewishness, in a particular community of Judaism, and in the family dynamic that reflects multiple levels of commitment.

Human beings cannot survive without nutrition. The symbolic equivalent in these examples extends that relationship to the social relationship, to the community at large, and to the spiritual entity within which those relationships are presumed to reside.

Symbols express complex ideas succinctly and economically, a property known as condensation, identified by Sigmund Freud in his analysis of dreams (1924). Edward Sapir (1934) describes symbols as highly condensed forms of behavior that substitute for direct action, allowing for the release of emotional tension in conscious or unconscious form. Sapir, like other researchers, notes that symbols are saturated with emotion.

Symbols also resolve or explain contradictions. With respect to myths (symbolic stories that explain human relationships), Claude Lévi-Strauss asserts that "the purpose of myth is to provide a logical model capable of overcoming a contradiction" (1963a, 229). In symbolic terms, contradiction adds to the power of the message. How else could one explain the power of the Virgin Mary to draw followers from a variety of cultural backgrounds? The contradiction of a virgin who is also a mother combines two innately powerful images that expand exponentially when brought together in the form of the Virgin Mary, a female figure who traverses the dangerous territory between human and divine and between the innocent and the aware. In the natural realm, a woman cannot become a mother without sexual knowledge. In the supernatural realm, exemplified by the Virgin Mary, a woman transcends the boundary between innocence (ignorance of sexual knowledge) and fecundity, which involves the production of a new human life. She is both innocent and fecund, and the product of that "marriage" is a child who transcends the chasm between human and divine. In the "logic" of symbols, contradiction is powerful because it invites the observer to transcend ordinary conceptual categories.

SIGNS AND SYMBOLS

Most anthropologists distinguish symbols from signs (e.g., Firth 1973, 65). Both symbols and signs communicate information through images, words, and behaviors. Signs, however, have only one possible meaning, whereas symbols, by definition, convey multiple levels of meaning at the same time. That is, symbols are multivocal (they speak with multiple voices), polysemic (they have multiple levels of meaning), or multivalent (they make multiple appeals). The distinction between sign and symbol was described by Carl Jung, who writes, "A symbol is an indefinite expression with many meanings, pointing to something not easily defined and therefore not fully known. But the sign always has a fixed meaning, because it is a conventional abbreviation for, or a commonly accepted indication of, something known" (1956, 124).

Both signs and symbols are important forms of communication because they convey information appropriate to a specific context. The sign ∞ indicates that the topic under consideration has no numerical limitation. On the other hand, the image of ouroboros, the snake swallowing its tail, also conveys the concept of infinity, but in this case, the infinity referred to has no finite designation. What, precisely, does it refer to? The answer is that the image is not precise. It approximates a variety of human experiences. It is a concise expression of concepts that cannot be stated precisely.

Victor Turner (1967, 26) builds on the distinction between signs and symbols to explain such complex cultural manifestations as myths, rituals, and the various forms of expressive culture. He notes, "Symbols . . . produce action. . . . Groups mobilize around them, worship before them, perform other symbolic activities near them, and add other symbolic objects to them, often to make composite shrines" (1967, 22).

Turner describes the many possible meanings of the *mudyi*, or milk tree, for the Ndembu: "At *Nkang'a*, the girl's puberty ritual, a novice is wrapped in a blanket and laid at the foot of a *mudyi* sapling" (1967, 20). This action conveys multiple meanings to the Ndembu, who say that the milk tree, which exudes white milky beads if its bark is scratched, stands for human breast milk. On an immediate level, the milk tree stands for the bond of nurturing between mother and child, but this special bond extends to all the mothers of the lineage, as well as to the founding ancestress of the Ndembu. Ndembu are matrilineal, which means membership in the group is traced through the female line.

> At one level of abstraction the milk tree stands for matriliny, the principle on which the continuity of Ndembu society depends. Matriliny governs succession to office and inheritance or property, and it vests dominant rights of residence in local units. More than any other principle of social organization it confers order and structure on Ndembu social life. (Turner 1967, 21)

By extension, the milk tree stands for tribal custom and for the bonds of interrelationship and interdependency that hold Ndembu society together. Rituals that incorporate milk tree symbolism are aimed at transmitting cultural knowledge.

> The child depends on its mother for nutriment; similarly, say the Ndembu, the tribesman drinks from the breast of tribal custom. Thus nourishment and learning are equated in the meaning content of the milk tree. I have often heard the milk tree compared to "going to school": the child is said to swallow instruction as a baby swallows milk." (Turner 1967, 22)

For Ndembu, the mudyi is a dominant symbol, as defined by Turner (1967, 31). It is called upon in a variety of contexts to represent values and principles central to the group.

Whereas Ndembu see the milk tree as representative of group solidarity, Turner notes that rituals incorporating milk tree symbolism make it clear that the mudyi "represents aspects of social differentiation and even opposition between the components of a society which ideally it is supposed to symbolize as a harmonious whole" (1967, 22). The "harmonious whole" represented by the milk tree is actually a conglomerate of individuals and subgroups who occupy different places in the social fabric and who, therefore, often have competing interests. The negotiation of conformity to cultural imagery and its apparent opposite, the negotiation of conflict, are not unique to the Ndembu. The use of symbols to promote a sense of conformity to stated values and reduce the disruption of conflict is common to all human groups.

METAPHORICAL AND METONYMICAL SYMBOLS

The meaning of symbols is arbitrary. That is, the meaning of a particular symbol is culturally assigned rather than inherent in the symbol. Still, there is a kind of apparently logical association between a symbol and its referent, the thing it represents. Ndembu, for example, see a logical association between mother's milk and the milky sap exuded by the mudyi tree. The eagle, one of the dominant symbols associated with the United States, is admired for its sharp vision and for its ability to bring down its prey. Similarly, the Christmas tree is rooted in the association between the evergreen tree and the continuation of life through the winter, when deciduous trees have lost their leaves and are apparently dead. The custom of lighting fires and decorating one's home with candles or strings of lights at this time—the winter solstice—is related to the fading of the light on the shortest day of the year in the northern hemisphere.

These are all symbols based on metaphor, or perceived similarity. Mother's milk is equated with the milky sap of the mudyi tree; the vision and prowess of the eagle are evoked when this symbol is associated with the United States; evergreen trees represent the aspiration for eternal life and the defiance of apparent death; and the light of fires and candles stands for the warmth and light of the sun, which is essential for life on earth.

Other symbols are based on metonymy, or contiguity, a conceptual process in which an object is symbolically connected to that with which it has once been in contact or of which it is a part. The linguist Nancy Bonvillain (1997) describes metonymy as a type of semantic transfer in which one entity stands for another based on their co-occurrence in context rather than on similarity of their attributes. In symbolic usage, magical practices that call for obtaining a lock of hair or nail parings from the person one wants to influence are based on metonymy. Relics of saints gain their power from having once been associated with holy persons. In the "logic" of metonymy, the part stands for the whole or the object stands for the entity with which it has been associated. In Christian symbols, the cross evokes not only the sacrifice of Christ but membership in a Christian organization and the Christian way of life in general.

George Lakoff writes, "Metonymy is one of the basic characteristics of cognition. It is extremely common for people to take one well-understood or easy-to-perceive aspect of something and use it to stand either for the thing as a whole or for some other aspect or part of it" (1987, 77).

Lakoff notes that metonymic models draw on culturally defined expectations associated with a specific entity. In the case of Christianity, for example, both the cross and the crown of thorns figure prominently in Christ's suffering and death. However, it is the cross, and not the crown of thorns, that stands for Christianity. The cross evokes Christ's suffering on behalf of humanity. The crown of thorns recalls the ridicule visited on Christ during his persecution. Thus, the cross invokes genuine nobility whereas the crown of thorns evokes meretricious royalty.

Though the eagle, the Christmas tree, the cross, and other such symbols appear to be "logical" or "natural," the selection of attributes to be symbolically emphasized is culturally determined. The association of the United States with the eagle draws on the eagle's vision and hunting skill rather than on its propensity for eating rodents. Also, in translating the eagle into a symbol, the bird is not portrayed as a predator but as a representative of power. The role of the field mouse is downplayed in the symbolic imagery, and the eagle is never portrayed with the tiny rodent in its talons. Instead, the eagle is often portrayed with a bundle of arrows in its talons. In nature, arrows would never attract the attention of this voracious predator. The integration of arrows with the image of an eagle visually emphasizes the eagle's power. Implicitly, however, enemies of the United States play the role of the scurrying rodent. By analogy, the United States devours only those countries that deserve to be eaten.

PURITY AND DANGER

Symbols organize our perception of reality by imposing order onto inchoate experience. In her book *Purity and Danger*, Mary Douglas asserts that disorder is seen as dirty and dangerous, whereas order is seen as clean and safe. She notes that "dirt is essentially disorder."

> There is no such thing as absolute dirt; it exists in the eye of the be-
> holder. If we shun dirt, it is not because of craven fear, still less dread or
> holy terror. Nor do our ideas about disease account for the range of our
> behavior in cleaning or avoiding dirt. Dirt offends against order. Elimi-
> nating it is not a negative movement, but a positive effort to organize the
> environment. (1966, 2)

The concept of dirt also extends into the social realm. Disorderly or inappropriate behavior—behavior that does not conform to the expectations of
a particular group—may be seen as unclean or dangerous. We may speak,
for example, of "airing our dirty linen in public." Clothing, which covers
our bodies appropriately in a public context, becomes "dirty" after it has
made contact with our bodies. The metaphor of "dirty linen" reflects a
North American concept of organic functions as being "dirty" and inorganic objects as being "clean." On another level, the inorganic objects called
clothing represent a mediating force—or metaphorical barrier—between
our private inclinations and the restrictions of public or social demands.

"The whole universe is harnessed to men's attempts to force one another into good citizenship" (Douglas 1966, 3). Just as clothing protects our
"private parts" from public view, social disorder is guarded against by clearly
demarcating categories.

> Ideas about separating, purifying, demarcating and punishing transgres-
> sions have as their main function to impose system on an inherently un-
> tidy experience. It is only by exaggerating the difference between within
> and without, above and below, male and female, with and against, that a
> semblance of order is created. (Douglas 1966, 4)

Though concepts of purity and danger are shaped by their social context,
they extend far beyond social distinctions, raising questions about the very
nature of being. Douglas writes, "Reflection on dirt involves reflection on
the relation of order to disorder, being to non-being, form to formlessness,
life to death. Wherever ideas of dirt are highly structured their analysis dis-
closes a play upon such profound themes" (1966, 5–6).

Douglas suggests that "dangerous things" are typically made secure
through imposition of taboos (ritual avoidance). For example, Jewish rules
for diet and conduct spelled out in the book of Leviticus involve taboos
that prevent mixing of categories. Douglas notes that the threefold classification delineated in Genesis—the earth, the waters, and the firmament—
are taken up in Leviticus as the basis for dietary rules concerning consumption of animals.

> In the firmament two-legged fowls fly with wings. In the water scaly fish swim with fins. On the earth four-legged animals hop, jump or walk. Any class of creatures which is not equipped for the right kind of locomotion in its element is contrary to holiness. Contact with it disqualifies a person from approaching the Temple. (Douglas 1966, 55)

Douglas notes that the basis of cleanliness is conformity to a conceptual category: "In general the underlying principle of cleanness in animals is that they shall conform fully to their class. Those species are unclean which are imperfect members of their class, or whose class itself confounds the general scheme of the world" (1966, 55).

Douglas adds that the Hebrew word *tebhel*, often mistranslated as "perversion," actually means "mixing" or "confusion." Leviticus 19:19 (New Revised Standard Version) states, "You shall keep my statutes. You shall not let your cattle breed with a different kind; you shall not sow your field with two kinds of seed; nor shall there come upon you a garment of cloth made of two kinds of stuff." Douglas summarizes as follows:

> We can conclude that holiness is exemplified by completeness. Holiness requires that individuals shall conform to the class to which they belong. And holiness requires that different classes of things shall not be confused.... Holiness means keeping distinct the categories of creation. It therefore involves correct definition, discrimination and order. (1966, 53)

Approaching the issue of order from another angle, Claude Lévi-Strauss (1963b) suggests that, beneath the surface gloss of culture and society, the deep structure of the human mind is universally the same. All people, he suggests, think in binary oppositions (paired opposites). Lévi-Strauss based his model on studies in linguistics, especially Roman Jakobson's model (1941) of a universal order of differentiation of sounds through distinctions between contrasting sets. Lévi-Strauss extended Jakobson's model of sound production to form his own model of concept production. In English, examples of contrasting conceptual sets include up-down, left-right, and sun-moon, among many others. In Chinese tradition, the yin-yang symbol represents the contrasting pairs of attributes associated with femaleness and maleness. The yin-yang symbol is a simplified model of the universe, which Chinese philosophers see as a balance between the feminine, the moon, completion, cold, darkness, material forms, and submission on the one hand and the masculine, the sun, creation, heat, light, heaven, and dominance on the other.[2]

Lévi-Strauss suggests that themes in myth represent a dialectic (or negotiation) between sets of opposing pairs. In his book *The Raw and the Cooked* (1964), Lévi-Strauss asserts that the concepts raw and cooked symbolize the universal human experience of negotiating the binary oppositions of nature and culture. In addition, the binary opposition of raw and cooked involves a third, mediating principle, the process that transforms the raw (primordial material) into the cooked (culture) or rotten (nature). As Edmund Leach summarizes this relationship, "Cooked food may be thought of as fresh raw food which has been transformed . . . by cultural means, whereas rotten food is fresh raw food which has been transformed by natural means" (1974, 26).

"NATURAL" SYMBOLS

If the meaning of symbols is arbitrary, why is it that symbols often seem to go so naturally with their referent, the thing or concept they stand for? Isn't it logical, for example, that an evergreen tree would be a symbol of eternal life whereas a deciduous tree, which loses its leaves and seems to die in winter, would not? Isn't it natural that water, which cleanses our bodies, might also purify our souls? Wouldn't that be logical to everyone?

Natural objects provide a matrix from which cultural symbols can be drawn. In principle, deciduous trees could provide the lesson that humans, like trees, return from apparent death. In fact, humans do not grow new leaves. They do not reappear after apparent death.

A folk tale of Yakima Indians, told by Bobby Lake-Thom (1997), explains why humans, unlike deciduous trees, do not return to the land of the living. At the beginning of creation, the story goes, humans and animals helped each other and learned from each other. When both humans and animals were visited by death, Coyote and Eagle decided to bring back the souls of the dead. "The dead shall not remain forever in the land of the deceased," Coyote said. "They are like the leaves that drop from the trees, brown and dead in the fall time; but they shall come back to life just like in the springtime, when the birds use their power to sing and bring back new life" (64).

Eagle and Coyote journeyed to the land of the dead and captured the souls of the dead, putting them in a large basket. The souls of the dead begged to be released from the basket, and over the objections of Eagle, Coyote opened the basket and released the souls of the dead. Moving like the wind, the souls quickly went back to the land of the dead. Eagle said,

"It is not yet autumn, the leaves are still falling, just as people die, so why don't we wait until spring [to bring back the souls of the dead]" (65–66). But Coyote was tired of his efforts to restore the souls of the dead to the living. "Let them stay in the land of the deceased forever," he said.

> So Coyote made the law that after people have died they shall never come back to life again. If he had not opened the basket and let the spirits out, the dead would have come to life every spring when the new leaves come to life and the flowers begin to bloom; and that is also why today the living humans and the dead are not supposed to be together. (66)

Mary Douglas notes that so-called natural symbols, and the meanings associated with them, develop out of our everyday experiences. "The more the symbol is drawn from the common fund of human experience, the more wide and certain its reception" (1966, 114). Douglas states that the body of living organisms is an especially potent source for symbols. She observes that human goals are reflected in treatment of the bodies of animals used in sacrifice. Among Dinka herders of Africa, for example, sacrificial animals are cut longitudinally through the sex organs to expiate a breach of the incest taboo. They are cut in half across the middle to celebrate a truce. Furthermore, the human body is a rich source of symbolism.

> The body is a model which can stand for any bounded system. Its boundaries can represent any boundaries which are threatened or precarious. The body is a complex structure. The functions of its different parts and their relation afford a source of symbols for other complex structures. (1966, 115)

Ultimately, Douglas writes, the various parts and functions of the body symbolize the collective body that is human society.

> The idea of society is a powerful image. It is potent in its own right to control or to stir men to action. This image has form; it has external boundaries, margins, internal structure. Its outlines contain power to reward conformity and repulse attack. There is energy in its margins and unstructured areas. (1966, 114)

The body is linked to social interaction linguistically in such common expressions as *head of state, the left hand doesn't know what the right hand is doing,* and *left-handed compliment.* Many ritual symbols draw on metaphors of the body, as in such practices as baptism and other forms of ritual cleansing. Just as the body is cleansed through bathing, the spirit is cleansed symbolically through being sprinkled or doused with water.

Rodney Needham (1972) noted that the possession of a body is common to all humans and that our experience of our bodies is subjective because it is the one thing in nature that is internally experienced. Fiona Bowie adds that the human body carries a particularly heavy symbolic load because "it is simultaneously experienced subjectively and objectively, it belongs both to the individual and to the wider social body" (2000, 41).

Douglas observes that any entity is most vulnerable at its margins. The human body is most vulnerable at its orifices; thus, any excretion from the body is viewed as dangerous: "Spittle, blood, milk, urine, faeces or tears by simply issuing forth have traversed the boundary of the body. So also have bodily parings, skin, nail, hair clippings and sweat" (1966, 121). These conceptually dangerous substances are typically surrounded by religious rituals and taboos, though attitudes and practices associated with them vary from one society to another. Some societies have ritual taboos associated with menstrual blood, whereas others do not. All forms of animal feces are considered "dirty" in the United States, but cow dung is used for fuel and plastering houses in some parts of India and among some African cattle herders. In the United States, "manure" becomes "fertilizer" when it is used to enrich soils for planting, and ammonia, which is derived from urine, is used for cleaning windows. In many societies, hair and nail clippings are used in magical rituals. Hair and nail clippings are metonymical symbols in that these objects are believed to have power over the body of which they were once a part.

The body is also associated with left-right symbolism. As the French sociologist Robert Hertz noted (1973 [1909]), most societies encourage right-handedness and discourage left-handedness. Most people in the world are right handed and, therefore, experience their right hand as normal and "in control." They experience their left hand as being "out of control." Thus, cross-culturally, the right hand is associated with the everyday world, and the left hand is associated with the supernatural, with danger, and with being out of control. In North America, someone who is seen as unpredictable, erratic, and perhaps dangerous is described as "coming from left field." In Hindu and Buddhist imagery, Tantrism is viewed as the "left-hand," or dangerous, path. Tantric rituals emphasize use of the left hand in conducting rites or performing other meaningful activities.

In Muslim practice, the left hand is never extended to another in greeting because it is used to clean oneself after bathroom functions. Similarly, in

Thai Buddhist culture, the left hand is considered inferior to the right, part of an overall conceptual model in which parts of the body are viewed as higher or lower, superior or inferior, and cleaner or dirtier. The value distinction is extended to one's place in society and to interactions with other people.

> The body attributes are very important in Thai culture: the head, hands, feet, person. The head is the most important part of the entire body. It should never be touched. The lower the head, the greater amount of respect given. The hand has two categories: the right being more acceptable and polite when giving or receiving and putting objects into the mouth; the left is generally regarded as of "lower class" because this is used for cleaning after restroom duty. In Thai culture, when receiving something, especially from an elder, both hands are used. Either hand should not be used to point at people, especially the forefinger. The feet are the lowest part of the body and the dirtiest ones. They are used for walking and never for pointing. Thai people would not step over any part of another person either when they are sitting up or lying down.[3]

In my study of professional athletes, I have noted that many athletes regularly observe left-right distinctions in their rituals (Womack 1982). Before a game, hockey players dress one side of the body first—socks, skates, knee pads, and so on—depending on what "worked" for them previously. Similarly, football players have their trainers tape either the left side or the right side first, depending on which side was taped first the last time the team won or the athlete had an unusually good game. Baseball players step over the foul line with either the left or the right foot first, again depending on which has "proved" successful in the past. The foul line is dangerous because it is an ambiguous space, one that determines whether a ball is foul or fair, and has the potential to determine the outcome of a game. Athletes who give priority to the left side are symbolically exerting control over the dangerous and unpredictable aspects of competition; those who give priority to the right side are emphasizing their connection with a safe, predictable, and orderly universe.

Just as some aspects of human life are universal, some symbols have similar associations cross-culturally. People everywhere experience birth, death, love, sexual desire, and the need for food and shelter, and these powerful aspects of human life find expression in compelling symbols. In addition, regardless of where we live or what we do for a living, we all experience the sun as a significant force. We experience the power of the sun in an immediate way when we walk from the shade into the light. Virtually all plants need the sun to survive and grow, and humans ultimately rely upon the ability of plants to convert light into food through the process of photosynthesis. The light and heat of the sun are important to all life everywhere on earth. Even the creatures of the deep are affected indirectly by the sun.

In his book *The Aesthetic Experience: An Anthropologist Looks at the Visual Arts*, Jacques Maquet describes a moment in which he contemplated the monumental tomb of Napoleon in the Church of Saint Louis of the Invalids. Maquet notes that it was an overcast day, and the somber tones of the tomb contrasted with the suffused golden light of the space. "Looking at Napoleon's tomb, I had forgotten Napoleon" (1986, 104).

Maquet compares the golden light under the dome with the sun: "It was an image of the sunlight when it shines outside, on Paris and elsewhere; it was a replica of the summer sun during a drab winter day. Visually, it was an exhilarating sunny day" (1986, 104). The quality of light negated the somber mood of the tomb, or perhaps the juxtaposition of light and dark enhanced its symbolic import. Maquet records his reflections: "It was a symbol of life. And indeed, the sunlight is what makes plants grow, what makes the Earth a warm and bright place. The sun is the source of life; it epitomizes life" (1986, 104).

The light and warmth of the sun are of such importance to life on earth that the sun is often personified in powerful anthropomorphic symbolism. In Hindu and Greek mythology, the sun is portrayed as a charioteer journeying across the sky. In Hinduism, the solar charioteer is Surya; in Greek mythology, he is Apollo. In Japanese Shinto mythology, the sun is portrayed as Amaterasu, the beautiful daughter of the divine progenitors of Japan, Izanami and Izanagi. Until the United States forced the Japanese emperor to give up all claims to divinity after World War II, Amaterasu was viewed as the founding mother of the Japanese imperial family line. Her emblem, the sun, is still the central feature on the Japanese flag.

Emiko Ohnuki-Tierney, who has studied the Ainu of northern Japan, suggests that "the warmth and brightness of the sun are more appreciated" in northern lands than in more southerly areas (1974, 106). Before World War II, Ainu foragers on what was then the northernmost island of Japan, Sakhalin, revered above all the mountain deities, of whom the most important was the bear. The most important sky deities were the sun (daytime moon) and the moon (dark moon), who were considered to be dual aspects of the same female deity. This deity was believed to mediate between the Ainu and other deities. Ohnuki-Tierney points out that the sun was important in drying fish for preservation, and "the moon provides the only source of light outside at night and therefore saves the lives of the people who must walk at night" (1974, 106).

Though the sun may be a benign force to people of the northern hemisphere, it can be less gentle in arid regions where few trees protect humans from its intense heat. The crescent moon and star associated with Islam have both symbolic and historical components. Historically, the crescent is associated with the founder of the Ottoman (Osmanli) Empire, Osman, who is said to have had a dream in which the crescent moon stretched from one end of the earth to another. Under the Ottomans, Constantinople was transformed into a wealthy capital and renamed Istanbul. The crescent may be associated with the god Diana on the west and the horns of the bull Nandi, the god Śiva's mount, on the east.

Early Muslim rulers did not have a symbolic icon; Islamic belief generally guards against representational images. During the time of the Prophet Muhammad, Islamic armies and caravans flew solid-colored flags of black, green, or white for purposes of identification.[4] Regardless of its origins, the symbol of crescent moon and star continues to resonate with those who have been exposed to the relentless heat of the sun and abrading effects of sandstorms. Symbols do not survive if they do not illuminate everyday experience. Symbols of the human and celestial bodies are natural not because their meaning is inherent in the object itself, nor because the meaning is contained in the history of a particular people, but because the symbolic objects help to define the experience of human beings in the natural order of things.

NOTES

1. Throughout this book I use the words *gods*, *heroes*, and *demons* as nongendered terms. The term *goddess* is a diminutive variation on the term *god*, which does not have gender. Where it is necessary to indicate gender, I use *female gods* or *male gods*.

2. See Richard Hooker's discussion of yin and yang principles at http://www.wsu.edu/~dee/CHPHL/YINYANG.HTM.

3. This model of Thai society was provided by Siririt Harris in her paper "Thai Ethnic Groups," written for my class taught in 1999.

4. See http://www.islam.about.com/library/weekly/aa060401a.htm.

2

HOW SYMBOLS ARE STUDIED

Symbols are intrinsically bound to human social life, having played a significant role in shaping the human experience in the comparatively brief history of *Homo sapiens*. Neanderthals, for whom there is a fossil record dating from at least 130,000 to 35,000 years ago, have been characterized as "the first hominids to systematically, and perhaps ritually, bury their dead" (Stein and Rowe 2000, 368; see also Fagan 1997, 374). Some Neanderthal corpses were covered with red ochre powder and/or interred with stone tools and animal remains, which may have been intended to equip the individual for an afterlife.

Though the Neanderthal data are controversial among some physical anthropologists and archaeologists, there is a clear record of symbolic expression associated with modern *Homo sapiens*. Early humans left a rich treasury of art dating from about 35,000 years ago, including figures carved from stone and bone, as well as paintings on rocks and in caves. They also decorated their tools and weapons with beautifully incised designs and realistic imagery.

Because these symbolic representations predate the development of writing, we cannot say with certainty what they meant to the people who compiled them, what the images were intended to communicate, or what entity—human, animal, or spirit—they were addressing. On some levels, it is ever thus with the study of symbols. Even when studying symbolic systems of people living today, interpretation of symbols is always approximate. Indeed, it is likely that even people who are expert in the use of symbols—shamans, priests, or sorcerers—cannot state precisely what a particular symbol is all about. Victor Turner notes that a study of symbols requires three classes of data: (1) the observable characteristics of a particular symbol, (2) interpretations offered by specialists and laypersons who use the symbol, and (3) significant social and behavioral contexts observed by the anthropologist (1967, 20).

The anthropological study of symbols is rooted in a number of analytical traditions, and it is only fair to pay homage to some of these. It is also well to note variations in the anthropological approach arising from differing theoretical positions within the discipline and from differing access to ethnographic data.

SYMBOLS AS SURVIVALS: THE NINETEENTH-CENTURY VIEW

Long before there was a symbolic anthropology, anthropologists were analyzing symbolic phenomena, including religion and magic. Nineteenth-century anthropologists attempted to determine the stages of human social evolution, especially to reconstruct what life might have been like for the earliest humans. These attempts were greatly hampered by the fact that no ethnographers were around to describe human society in its early stages. Even had there been acute observers of the social scene when humans emerged as a distinct species, there was no writing system with which to record their observations.

Since ethnography as a systematic methodological and analytical tool for describing particular social groups did not develop until the turn of the twentieth century, most nineteenth-century anthropologists generally were not aware of the importance of systematic observation and data collection for analysis. Their data primarily came from travelers' tales of their wondrous adventures and from the anthropologists' speculation about what early human society must have been like, based on their own experience of European society in the nineteenth century. Some anthropologists, including the American anthropologist Lewis Henry Morgan, conducted surveys asking colonial administrators about the customs of people under their domination. Nineteenth-century social evolutionists also drew on available records of early Greek and Roman societies. Though their ideas contributed greatly to later anthropological theory, nineteenth-century anthropologists were biased by their assumption that the English and European society of their day represented the pinnacle of biological, cultural, and social evolution.

An important exception to the nineteenth-century pattern of armchair anthropology was the formation of the first anthropological society, the *Société des Observateurs de l'Homme*, in Paris in 1800. The society under-took a scientific expedition to study indigenous people of the south coast of Australia. Even in this case, the researchers were biased by their assumption that "civilized" Europeans were intellectually and morally superior to the "savages," who were presumed to be superior in health, strength, and general physical perfection. One member of the expedition, François Péron, proposed to test his hypothesis that "[Europeans'] moral perfection must be in inverse ratio to [Australian aborigines'] physical perfection" (quoted in Langness 1987, 9).

Even by that time, Joseph Marie de Gérando had written a guide to fieldwork, *Considerations on the diverse methods to follow in the observations of savage peoples*, which anticipated later approaches in several ways. De Gérando considered careful observation of specific groups to be the essen-tial basis for comparisons between groups, which could then be used to de-rive general laws of human behavior. He also advocated learning the lan-guage of "savages" and becoming their "fellow-citizens." In other words, De Gérando advocated taking the insider perspective, a hallmark of later an-thropological research. In addition, De Gérando advised the technique of making numerous observations and avoiding the assumption of conformity to a single type (Langness 1987, 9; see also Stocking 1968, 23–24).

In the same way that an embryo anticipates the organism it is to be-come, these early attempts to understand the human experience are re-markable for their accuracy in framing the issues that later shaped the field of symbolic anthropology.

MYTHOLOGY AND PREHISTORY

The Swiss scholar J. J. Bachofen viewed ancient Greek mythology as a sym-bolic record of human life in its earliest stages. Bachofen's best-known work today is *Das Mutterrecht (Mother Right)*, originally published in German in 1861. In it, Bachofen examined the writings of Greek historians and poets, finding in them evidence of a matrilineal system of inheritance stemming from an earlier time. Based on these writings, Bachofen concluded that hu-man societies developed from a primitive matriarchy in which women held power, descent was reckoned through the female line, and religious life was based on worship of a female deity. Bachofen then extended this view of a primitive matriarchy, drawn from one early Greek society, to all of human evolution, based on what he called "the universal qualities of human nature" (1967, 71). According to Bachofen, this earlier, "more primitive way of life" was displaced by classical Greek culture, characterized by patrilineal inheritance, a political system in which males hold power, and a religion ordered around the father principle.

As have many other scholars, Bachofen confused matriliny (descent or inheritance) with matriarchy (a form of political organization). Bachofen also applied concepts derived only from Greek and Roman history and mythology to all human groups. In addition, he drew conclusions about human behavior without observing actual humans behaving, that is, in the absence of ethnography. In line with other nineteenth-century scholars, he also classified some groups as "more primitive" than others.

Bachofen's continuing contribution to anthropology is the idea that we can learn *something* about human groups by studying their mythology, which contains a symbolic record of their views of the universe, the nature of human relations, and the cycle of human life. It is difficult to determine what that *something* is, however. Mythology is a conceptual model rather than a literal history. Ann Grodzins Gold (1993) notes that the violent power of women expressed in Hindu mythology does not translate into powerful women in Indian society, nor are ordinary Hindu women able to express anger in the form of violence. Instead, Grodzins Gold writes, these myths may reflect the *desire* of Hindu women to rebel against male authority rather than their *power* to do so.

John McLennan, Bachofen's contemporary, also used classical authors to deal with symbolic issues. Unlike Bachofen, McLennan used travelers' accounts of non-Europeans, including observations of people of central Africa, the Americas, India, and the Pacific Islands (Hays 1958, 37). McLennan was interested in symbolic forms of bride capture, in which the groom is expected to make a great show of stealing his bride from her family and the bride is expected to make a great show of resisting. McLennan suggested that this ritual could have developed from practices in an earlier time when descent was reckoned through the female line, and a scarcity of women, due to female infanticide, forced men to compete for wives.

Like Bachofen, McLennan assumed a link between symbolic accounts and actual behavior. Similarly, McLennan could not base his analysis on a systematic comparison of the relationship between symbols and social interaction because he did not have data on the behaviors of early humans. Researchers in the social sciences have noted that self-described accounts often vary from actual behavior, even in reports of such mundane activities as what one did during the day, because descriptions typically are biased toward idealistic models. Symbolic stories are especially biased toward idealistic models because their intent is to provide models for behavior or to serve as cautionary tales designed to steer hearers of the story away from behavior considered to be undesirable.

Even though Bachofen's and McLennan's speculative models of early human groups, based on their symbolic expression in myth and ritual, cannot be verified through systematic data collection, these scholars made important contributions to the study of symbols, if only by providing ideas for later scholars to explore in more depth after the collection of more ethnographic and archaeological data.

"PRIMITIVE MENTALITY"

Unlike Bachofen and McLennan, E. B. Tylor had traveled outside Europe. Born into an affluent English Quaker family, Tylor was prevented by the threat of tuberculosis from taking up his more likely career in the family brass foundry. Instead, as a young man, Tylor was sent on a tour of North America in search of a climate more favorable for his health. This proved to be fortuitous both for Tylor and for anthropology since it provided an opportunity for the incipient scholar to tour Cuba and Mexico. In fact, Tylor's first book, published in 1861, *Anahuac or Mexico and the Mexicans, Ancient and Modern*, was based on his travels.

In his book *Primitive Culture* (1871), Tylor formulated the concept of *survivals* to explain certain practices that seemed inexplicable from a practical standpoint. Tylor believed that rituals and religious beliefs originally had a practical purpose but became meaningless when the social context changed. He viewed magic and divination, including palmistry and astrology, as survivals of early forms of religious belief.

Tylor suggested that people in earlier evolutionary stages do not distinguish between a thing and the image of a thing, a characteristic he called "primitive mentality." Thus, according to Tylor, early humans believed that a thing or a person could be controlled by manipulating an image of the thing or person. Symbolic anthropologists now describe this conceptual process as metaphor and do not view it as characteristic of a more primitive or earlier type of thought. In fact, the ability to process metaphors is a sophisticated skill, one that may have developed long after humans acquired the ability to make precise references to physical objects and events.

Tylor observed that there is a widespread tendency to personify inanimate objects, that is, to endow them with life and human feelings. As an example, Tylor noted an old English law that required that any object or animal involved in the death of a man—such as a cartwheel that ran over him or a horse that kicked him—be sold to the poor as an indirect offering to God. This requirement was based on the idea that these objects were guilty of the death of the man. Similarly, according to old German custom, when the master or mistress of the house died, a "telling of the bees" was required. All the household animals and produce from the gardens or fields had to be told of the death. In the former case, guilt was assigned to the object or animal responsible for the death. In the latter case, household objects and animals were believed to share the emotions and fate of the people of the household.

Tylor considered these beliefs to be characteristic of an earlier stage of evolution. He viewed the widespread beliefs that inanimate objects have an animating spirit (or soul) as survivals of the earliest form of religion, which he called *animism*. Tylor theorized that a belief in spirits that animate people and objects derived from early speculations about the nature of human experience, specifically the processes of dreaming and dying. Tylor noted that dreaming involves a journey of the mind that is not shared by the body. Death involves dramatic, observable changes in the human body. Tylor suggested that the earliest religions sought to explain where people go when they dream and what causes the dying human body to undergo such dramatic changes.

Tylor exerted a major influence over a Glasgow-born scholar later knighted as Sir James Frazer. After reading Tylor's *Primitive Culture*, Frazer undertook an encyclopedic study of mythology and folklore from all parts of the world. In his book *The Golden Bough*, Frazer concluded that magic is based on the conceptual principle of sympathy, which is based on the assumption that "things act on each other at a distance through a secret sympathy" (1922, 14). Subsumed under the general principle of sympathetic magic are two conceptual processes, which Frazer calls *laws of thought: homeopathic* or *imitative magic* and *contagious magic*. Imitative magic is based on the idea that "like produces like, or an effect resembles its cause" (1922, 12), and contagious magic is based on the idea that "things which have once been in contact with each other continue to act on each other at a distance after the physical contact has been severed" (1922, 12).

The vodou doll is an example of imitative magic since the doll is made in the likeness of the human it represents. In addition, vodou dolls often include hair or nail clippings from the person the maker desires to influence, and the magical power perceived to be in these objects is based on the principle of contagion. In more contemporary terms, imitative magic is a form of symbolic behavior based on metaphor; contagious magic is a form of symbolic behavior based on metonymy.

MYTHOPOETIC, OR "NONRATIONAL," THOUGHT

"Primitive mentality" continues to be studied as *mythico-religious* or *mythopo-etic* thought, and it may well be that the essential error of these early theorists was not their formulation of mythopoetic thought but their assumption that it represented a primitive stage of human development. The linguist Ernst Cassirer rejected the idea that nonrational thought is a "mental defect," noting that what he calls *naive realism*, "which regards the reality of objects as something directly and unequivocally given" (1946, 6), is also based on false assumptions about the nature of our apprehension of experience.

> All mental processes fail to grasp reality itself, and in order to represent it, to hold it at all, they are driven to the use of symbols. But all symbolism harbors the curse of mediacy; it is bound to obscure what it seeks to reveal.... Even knowledge can never reproduce the true nature of things as they are, but must frame their essence as "concepts." (Cassirer 1946, 7)

Douglass Price-Williams suggests that the anthropological debate over mythopoetic thought reflects a bias, grounded in European philosophy, in which thought (or rationality) is distinguished from emotion, with the former being valued and the latter being devalued.

> I am going to suggest that mythopoetic thought is really not thought, at least as we understand it. . . . Moving away from the narrower term *thought* to the wider term *understanding* . . . allows us to pay attention to tacit behavior that requires the attentions of sociolinguists and discourse analysts insofar as much of it is carried in prosody, in pauses between utterances, in jokes and puns, and the like. It also requires the skills of the ethnographer for observing gestures and the context of communication. (Price-Williams 1999, 29; italics in the original)

Understood as the basis for art, music, drama, and other forms of cultural expression, mythopoetic thought is neither primitive nor a relic of an earlier stage of evolution. Rather, mythopoesis allows us to conceptualize experiences that cannot be reduced to literal description or unidimensional analysis.

PSYCHOANALYTIC APPROACHES

Contemporaneous with nineteenth-century social anthropologists and influenced by them, the psychologist Sigmund Freud identified symbols as a form of communication between the unconscious and conscious aspects of the mind. Freud based his psychoanalytic approach on his view of the importance of the unconscious as a repository for repressed memories and as a source of information for addressing and resolving conflicts. According to Freud, information is repressed if it threatens our construction of our social selves.

Psychoanalytical theory views individual psychology as deriving from the dynamic tension among the id, the ego, and the superego. The id is the repository of unconscious impulses; the superego develops from the internalization of cultural norms; and the ego mediates between the two. For Freud, impulses arising from the id are predominantly sexual.

> Every time we should be led by analysis to the sexual experiences and desires of the patient, and every time we should have to affirm that the symptom served the same purpose. This purpose shows itself to be the gratification of sexual wishes; the symptoms serve the purpose of sexual gratification for the patient; they are a substitute for satisfactions which he does not obtain in reality. (1924, 308)

In the process of socialization, according to Freud, children learn that the activities that provide them with the greatest pleasure—sucking, masturbating, and excreting—are considered by others to be abhorrent. Freud calls the energy arising from repression of the sex drive *libido*.

Repressed sexual impulses may be expressed in disguised form as symbols. Just as Freud considered repressed sexual impulses to be the source of psychological conflicts, he interpreted symbols as oblique references to sexuality. He considered containers to be symbolic of the vagina, cylindrical objects to be phallic symbols (referring to the penis), and vigorous activity such as a galloping horse to be symbolic of the sex act. In one case, Freud suggests that a woman symbolically expressed her desire to protect her virginity in her dreams by "trying to prevent the falling and breaking of vessels" (1924, 310). Since containers represent the vagina in Freudian symbolic imagery, a woman who tries to guard against the "breaking of vessels" is symbolically guarding against the destruction of her hymen.

THE UNCONSCIOUS AND CREATIVITY

Carl Jung presented a broader, and in some way more controversial, perspective on the relationship between symbols and unconscious impulses. According to Jung, the unconscious is the source of creativity and healing, as well as the repository of unresolved conflicts. Jung's concept of libido extends well beyond the sexual realm: "Libido is appetite in its natural state. From the genetic point of view it is bodily needs like hunger, thirst, sleep, and sex, and emotional states or affects, which constitute the essence of libido" (1956, 135–36).

Both Jung and Freud considered that myths could be analyzed as symbolic representations of libidinal impulses on the societal level, much as dreams could be analyzed as symbolic representations of conflict on the individual level. Unlike Freud, Jung asserted that controls over biological impulses are universally encoded in symbolic form in the human psyche: "Except when motivated by external necessity, the will to suppress or repress the natural instincts, or rather to overcome their predominance . . . and lack of co-ordination . . . derives from a spiritual source" (1956, 157).

Jung called the "spiritual source" of controls over libidinous impulses "the numinous [i.e., supernatural or mysterious] primordial images" found on a societal level in magic, religion, and political ideologies. Where these "collective representations" are lacking, Jung writes, "their place is immediately taken by all sorts of private idiocies and idiosyncrasies, mania, phobias, and daemonisms" (1956, 156). In other words, according to Jung, private demons rush in to fill the void left by a lack of public gods, heroes, and demons.

Jung also suggested that the power of the numinous images is inherent in the images themselves and beyond the control of the individual: "The images, ideas, beliefs, or ideals operate through the specific energy of the individual, which he cannot always utilize at will for this purpose, but which seems rather to be drawn out of him by the images" (1956, 157).

Jung's view of the unconscious developed in part because he was more familiar with the religious traditions of other cultures than Freud was. Jung studied Hinduism, Buddhism, and Taoism, as well as anthropological accounts of religions from other cultures. Freud based his views of religion primarily on the Judeo-Christian tradition, which, in its most commonly understood form, centers on a supreme male God, the symbolic Father. It is also more restrictive in its approach to sexuality than other religious traditions. Consequently, Freud saw religion as a restrictive and inhibiting force acting as the enforcing arm of the superego or internalized father. In *Civilization and Its Discontents*, Freud writes,: "I cannot think of any need in childhood as strong as the need for a father's protection," thus contradicting his statement earlier in the same book that an infant's first and most compelling desire is the mother's breast. Freud connects the child's need for a strong, protective father with the need for a strong, protective Providence: "The common man cannot imagine this Providence otherwise than in the figure of an enormously exalted father" (1961, 21).

The concept of a supreme male God and severe restrictions on female sexuality are linked to the nomadic sheepherder tradition in which they developed. Patriliny is cross-culturally linked to the need to control female sexuality as a means of preventing male outsiders from symbolically invading the lineage. The semen of external males "pollutes" the lineage by diffusing control of lineage males over their rights of inheritance. The power of the supreme male God is a magnification of the power of the male clan head over his followers.

THE GENERATIVE SOURCE

Freud was unaware that concepts of the supreme force in the universe are commonly represented symbolically as a generative mother, as a nongendered force, or as a generative source. Jung, who was familiar with the fertility symbolism of Hinduism and other agricultural traditions, saw the potential of religious symbolism for representing growth and creativity. Thus, while Freud considered containers such as baskets to represent female sexuality, Jung saw them as also representing the generative force of the mother. In Jungian psychology, images of the mother include containers, the sea, caves, generative trees, a mother personification, and the city: "The city is a maternal symbol, a woman who harbours the inhabitants in herself like children" (1956, 208). By extension, maternal images are symbols of transformation representing death and rebirth. Individuals whose dreams express imagery of the mother were considered by Jung to be going through a period of transition, psychologically equivalent to death and rebirth.

Jung considered symbols of the mother to be archetypes, universal symbols that exert an irresistible attraction: "The archetype, as a glance at the history of religious phenomena will show, has a characteristically numinous effect, so that the subject is gripped by it as though by an instinct. What is more, instinct itself can be restrained and even overcome by this power" (1956, 158).

Both Jung's concept of the archetype and his assumption that humans have instincts have been challenged by more recent scholars. It is instructive to note, however, that the *mandala*, or sacred circle, which Jung identifies as an archetype representing the idealized self, is essential to the symbolism of many religions. Jung took the name of this symbol from the iconography of

Tibetan Buddhism, in which the mandala is typically represented as a square within a circle. In Tibetan symbolism, the mandala represents the cosmos on a number of levels, from the personal to the universal. Similarly, the yin-yang symbol of Chinese philosophy represents the harmonious balance of female and male energy in the universe. In other religions, the circle is used in rituals as a source of protection and healing or as representative of the community of believers.

MEDUSA'S HAIR

Gananath Obeyesekere applied the psychoanalytic model directly to the anthropological study of symbols in his book *Medusa's Hair* (1981). Obeyesekere sought to explain the importance of matted hair for devotees at the pilgrimage site of Kataragama in Sri Lanka. Obeyesekere writes, "Here in the month of Asala (generally in July), ecstatics, mystics, and penitents belonging to all religions and coming from different parts of the country gather to pay their homage to the great god of the place" (1981, 2). Of particular note in Obeyesekere's study are the priests and priestesses who congregate at the site to renew their power, "generally by walking over the burning coals of the Kataragama fire walk or by performing various *pujas* [ritual offerings] to the god" (1981, 2).

In his case studies of priests and priestesses taking part in the ceremonies at Kataragama, Obeyesekere observes that devotion to the god, and its expression in the visible symbol of matted hair as a boon from the god, allows these individuals to resolve dilemmas in their personal lives and family relationships. He notes that, in classical psychoanalysis, patients construct fantasies aimed at resolving their psychic conflict and integrating their personalities. Obeyesekere calls this "the so-called private symbolism," adding, "But fantasy can produce only self-communication, not communication with others, for the ideational system of the patient is not a shared one" (1981, 160). To be successful, the inner integration must be matched to an outer integration with society. This is doomed to failure, however, since the private fantasy of the seriously ill patient does not match that of the society.

> Successful integration of the patient ideally must occur on all three fronts: personality, culture, and society. This is also the goal of the symbol systems [shared by the priests and priestesses at the Kataragama pilgrimage site]. The link between personality and society is often via the cultural symbol system. (Obeyesekere 1981, 160)

The matted hair of the priests and priestesses at Kataragama provides an external mark of favor from the god, and that mark accords with cultural symbols. The culturally recognized "mark of favor" allows the individuals to achieve their social goals through congruence between their personalities and cultural expectations regarding their behavior.

ANOTHER PSYCHOLOGICAL APPROACH

Though psychoanalytic theory has exerted the primary psychological influence on the anthropological study of symbols, other branches of psychology have also played important roles. A study by Leon Festinger, H. W. Riecken, and H. Schachter, described in the book *When Prophecy Fails* (1956), has exerted a great influence on anthropological studies of new religious movements. These psychologists noted the reactions of followers when the doomsday prophecy of a charismatic religious leader failed to come true. Festinger and colleagues observed that followers who were with the group when the prophecy failed accepted the explanations of the leader and remained members of the religious movement. Those who were alone when the prophecy failed to materialize in the physical destruction of the world lost their faith in the religious leader and left the movement. This study is important not only for what it has to say about revitalization and millenarian movements, which are aimed at bringing about social change, but for its usefulness in explaining the dynamics of belief in cultural symbols and commitment to group processes.

DURKHEIM AND BRITISH SOCIAL ANTHROPOLOGISTS

Whereas psychologists focus on factors influencing the conceptual system of the individual and psychological anthropologists focus on the interrelationship between the individual and the group, social anthropologists aim their analyses at the level of the group. As is evident from chapter 1 and as will become more evident in later chapters, much of the approach of this book follows the social anthropological model. This is primarily because the social anthropological approach was the dominant model guiding the development of symbolic anthropology in the latter half of the twentieth century and because anthropologists following this model placed great emphasis on collecting ethnographic data relating to group dynamics.

The analysis of symbols in their social context can be traced to the French sociologist Emile Durkheim, whose book *The Elementary Forms of the Religious Life* was published in English in 1915. Durkheim defined religion as an essentially social phenomenon.

> A society whose members are united by the fact that they think in the same way in regard to the sacred world and its relations with the profane world, and by the fact that they translate these common ideas into common practices, is what is called a Church. In all history, we do not find a single religion without a Church. (Durkheim 1915, 59)

Based on his analysis of beliefs and practices of Australian Aborigines regarding their totemic ancestors, Durkheim argued that religion represents the collective power of the group. In the case of the Aborigines, the relevant group is the clan, the kin group that traces descent from a totemic ancestor. "Since religious force is nothing other than the collective and anonymous forces of the clan, and since this can be represented in the mind only in the form of the totem, the totemic emblem is like the visible body of the god" (Durkheim 1915, 253).

Durkheim's views on the primacy of the social group greatly influenced A. R. Radcliffe-Brown, a chief architect of twentieth-century British social anthropology. Radcliffe-Brown asserted that religion and ritual reinforce the stability of the social order by clearly defining and reinforcing status and roles within the group, especially by validating the authority of group leaders. Radcliffe-Brown's emphasis on factors that promote the stability of the social group influenced an entire generation of British social anthropologists, including Victor Turner. These anthropologists produced studies, especially focused on African symbolic systems, that formed the basis of what later became symbolic anthropology.

MALINOWSKI AND THE "CALCULATING MAN"

Bronislaw Malinowski, the anthropologist who is credited with developing the method of participant observation, might well be astonished to discover himself among the pioneers in symbolic anthropology. Yet he well deserves this place. Like Radcliffe-Brown, Malinowski asserted that social institutions, including religion and magic, serve a function, a theoretical position Malinowski defined as *functionalism*. Unlike Radcliffe-Brown, Malinowski believed that the function of social institutions was to serve human needs, both biological and psychological. According to Malinowski, social institutions provide a framework within which individuals can negotiate to meet their needs. This is the "calculating man" model, or as Malinowski puts it, in discussing religion and magic, "rational mastery by man of his surroundings" (1954, 25).

In discussing the use of gardening magic by Trobriand Islanders, Malinowski notes that the success of gardeners depends "upon their extensive knowledge of the classes of the soil, of the various cultivated plants, of the mutual adaptation of these two factors, and, last but not least, upon their knowledge of the importance of accurate and hard work" (1954, 27). Though Trobrianders possess technical knowledge and skill in gardening, work in the gardens is always accompanied by the use of magic to protect against "various kinds of disaster, blight, unseasonable droughts, rains, bushpigs and locusts [which] would destroy the unhallowed garden made without magic" (1954, 28). Work is used to deal with the well-known conditions of gardening; magic is used to cope with "unaccountable and adverse influences, as well as the great unearned increment of fortunate coincidence" (1954, 29).

Malinowski's work is significant for the anthropological study of symbols on three levels: (1) He rejected the idea, prevalent among nineteenth-century social evolutionists, that "primitives" think differently from "civilized" humans. Instead, he emphasized the universality of thought processes underlying the use of symbols. (2) He demonstrated the compatibility of symbolic behavior with pragmatic, technical behavior, noting that both are important in conducting human affairs.[1] (3) He provided sufficient data on the social and psychological context of symbols as manifested in myths, rituals, and dreams—as well as Trobriander explanations for their behavior—to allow later anthropologists to build on his work.

LANGUAGE AND THE CREATION OF SYMBOLIC UNIVERSES

The Dogon philosopher-shaman Ogotemmêli describes the world as having been created through a series of three Words. The first Word came in the form of vapor or moisture contained in plants covering the private parts of the earth, symbolically represented as a woman who gave birth to the Nummo, male and female twins who together represent the perfection of creation: "When Nummo speaks, what comes from his mouth is a warm vapour which conveys, and itself constitutes, speech" (Griaule 1965, 20). The second Word came in the form of regeneration, the creative process of gestation in the womb that gives differentiation between female and male, and eventually to the rebirth that transforms humans from earthbound beings into the world of spirit. The third Word gave rise to the cosmological order, which was created when ancestors who had been transformed into the world of spirit "came down to earth again in a vast apparatus of symbols, in which was included a third and definitive Word necessary for the working of the modern world" (Griaule 1965, 30).

Thus, Ogotemmêli, an African philosopher of the western Sudan, identified symbols and language as the essential ingredient of creation, of the cosmological and social order, and of the essence of being human. Ogotemmêli is not alone in drawing this link among language, creativity, the phenomenal world, and the ultimate generative source. In Christian tradition, the apostle John conveys a similar message: "In the beginning was the Word, and the Word was with God, and the Word was God. The same was in the beginning with God. All things were made by him; and without him was not any thing that was made. In him was life; and the life was the light of men" (John 1:1–4; except where otherwise noted, all biblical quotations are from the King James Version).

Linguists have similarly noted the relationship between language and the human experience.

> The original bond between the linguistic and the mythico-religious consciousness is primarily expressed in the fact that all verbal structures appear as also mythical entities, endowed with certain mythical powers, that the Word, in fact, becomes a sort of primary force, in which all being and doing originate. In all mythical cosmogonies, as far back as they can be traced, this supreme position of the Word is found. (Cassirer 1946, 45)

The linguistic component of the study of symbols has produced a rich body of literature on the relationship of language to thought, on the essential properties of human language, on the use of language to negotiate conceptual and social space, and on variability in the social context of language use. It would be impossible to encapsulate this vast body of analysis in so small a space. It is appropriate, however, to summarize the writings of a few linguists to illustrate how much they have contributed to this book.

LANGUAGE AND SYMBOLS

Language and symbols share a number of characteristics, including the fact that both are systems of communication. Though there is an overlap between language and symbols, the two types of communication differ in form and function. Edward Sapir describes characteristics that "apply to all languages, living or extinct, written or unwritten." "Language is primarily a system of phonetic symbols for the expression of communicable thought and feeling. In other words, the symbols of language are differentiated products of the vocal behavior which is associated with the larynx of the higher mammals" (1949, 2).

As Sapir notes, language is verbal. Symbols communicate not only by means of words but also in images and behavior. In fact, symbols communicate primarily through imagery. For example, the Christian cross communicates multiple levels of information about the history, values, and appropriate conduct for Christians, as well as the relationship of human beings to divine beings. The cross also communicates information about what it means to belong to a particular Christian group and distinguishes members of the in-group from outsiders. The crucifix, on which Christ is depicted in the act of crucifixion, is part of the symbolic repertoire of Roman Catholics. However, it is rejected by many other Christian groups, who object to what they view as "worshipping an idol." For these other Christian groups, the cross without a representation of Christ is an object of reverence, but the crucifix is an example of a religious idol.

Because language is verbal, it has the power to communicate information precisely and succinctly. Through the use of images, symbols have the power to evoke an emotional response by communicating on multiple levels simultaneously. As will be discussed in later chapters, religious and artistic symbols speak volumes without saying a word.

The issue of whether art is a language has been discussed at length by art theorists. Art is certainly a symbol, as has long been recognized, but is it language? The question was addressed directly in a conversation between Marc Trujillo and Rackstraw Downes, both Yale-trained artists. When Trujillo referred to painting as a "language," Downes retorted that art is definitely not a language: "When two writers write the same words, it *is* the same; when two artists paint the same thing, it is different." Trujillo later came to agree with Downes, noting, "A Zuburan lemon is not the same as a Cézanne lemon" (personal communication 2002).

METAPHOR AND METONYMY

Language and symbols overlap in the area of metaphor and metonymy, concepts introduced in chapter 1. George Lakoff and Mark Johnson write of metaphor, "Metaphor is pervasive in everyday life, not just in language, but in thought and action. Our ordinary conceptual system, in terms of which we both think and act, is fundamentally metaphorical in nature" (1980, 3). The authors assert that metaphor is essential for the conduct of human life.

> The concepts that govern our thought are not just matters of the intellect. They also govern our everyday functioning, down to the most mundane details. Our concepts structure what we perceive, how we get around in the world, and how we relate to other people. Our conceptual system thus plays a central role in defining our everyday realities. (Lakoff and Johnson 1980, 3)

Lakoff and Johnson also state that the conceptual processes of metaphor and metonymy are fundamentally different. Metaphor is based on reasoning by analogy or comparison. Metonymy identifies a significant category for reference: "[Metonymy] serves the function of providing understanding.... Which part we pick out determines which aspect of the whole we are focusing on" (1980, 36). Lakoff and Johnson give as an example the statement, "We need some *good heads* on the project." The term *good heads* singles out a part of the human anatomy that conceptually represents "intelligent people." We might equally single out another part of the anatomy for metonymical imagery, as in the line from a poem by Edna St. Vincent Millay: "I am not resigned to the shutting away of loving hearts in the hard ground."[2]

Parallels between the concepts of metaphor and metonymy and Frazer's idea of imitative and contagious magic illustrate the idea that, though scholars from different disciplines or subdisciplines may disagree on the appropriate approach to studying symbols, the entity on which they focus their study remains consistent through time. In fact, scholars from different theoretical perspectives agree to a remarkable extent on the essential nature and properties of symbols.

LANGUAGE AND MYTH

In discussing the relationship between language and myth, Cassirer draws on Max Müller's observation that myth is "nothing but the darkening shadow which language throws upon thought" (quoted in Cassirer 1946, 9). Cassirer adds that myth takes on a dynamic of its own that eclipses our experience of "what we commonly call the immediate reality of *things*, so that even the wealth of empirical, sensuous experience pales before it" (1946, 9; italics in the original).

> Thus the special symbolic forms are not imitations, but *organs* of reality, since it is solely by their agency that anything real becomes an object for intellectual apprehension, and as such is made visible to us. . . . Any symbolic form . . . language, art, or myth . . . is a particular way of seeing, and carries within itself its particular and proper source of light. (Cassirer 1946, 8–11; italics in the original)

The idea that the purpose of symbols is to "make visible" aspects of the human experience not available to ordinary perception is not restricted to Western scholars. Victor Turner notes that "in discussing their symbols with [the Ndembu people of Zambia], one finds them constantly using the term *ku-sola*, 'to make visible' or 'to reveal'" (1967, 48). The term *ku-sola* is associated with hunting, in which the term *ku-jikijila* means "'to blaze a trail,' by cutting marks on a tree with one's ax or by breaking and bending branches to serve as guides back from the unknown bush to known paths" (1967, 48). Turner adds, "A symbol, then, is a blaze or landmark, something that connects the unknown with the known" (1967, 48). The concept of making something visible is extended to the *musoli* tree, which attracts game animals such as duiker. Parts of the musoli tree are used in rituals to aid hunting, to make women fertile (to "make children visible"), to heal, and to bring rain (to "make rain visible").

PHILOSOPHY

It could be argued with justification that all branches of philosophy have made intellectual contributions to the study of anthropology in general and to the anthropological study of symbols in particular. In fact, a number of anthropologists have traced the origins of anthropology to Greek philosophers. T. K. Penniman writes, "The first, and by far the longest period in the history of anthropology, extends from the time of the Greek historians, philosophers, and naturalists, until the thirties of the [nineteenth] century" (1965, 23). It is beyond the scope of this book to explore in depth the contribution of philosophers to the anthropological study of symbols. Instead, we will focus on the contribution of one modern philosopher, Susanne K. Langer, who has helped to stimulate contemporary studies of symbols.

Langer asserts that what she calls the "dying philosophical epoch" has been "eclipsed by a tremendously active age of science and technology" (1979, 13). A science based in empiricism places a primary value on conclusions drawn from sensory data, thus representing a shift in the idea of what constitutes evidence. Langer observes that a philosophy based on logic cannot compete with a system of knowledge based on empirical observation. "A passion for observation displaced the scholarly love of learned dispute, and quickly developed the experimental technique that kept humanity supplied thrice over with facts" (1979, 15). The idea emerged that science represents truth whereas philosophy is based on speculation, in spite of the fact that all sensory data are subject to interpretation. "The problem of observation is all but eclipsed by the problem of *meaning*. And the triumph of empiricism in science is jeopardized by the surprising truth that *our sense-data are primarily symbols*" (Langer 1979, 21; italics in the original). Thus, she concludes, philosophy can survive only by focusing on the study of symbols.

Langer follows the model of anthropologists discussed in chapter 1 in distinguishing symbols from signs. She notes the importance of symbols in conveying meanings that go well beyond objective information.

> A concept is all that a symbol really conveys. But just as quickly as the concept is symbolized to us, our own imagination dresses it up in a private, personal *conception*, which we can distinguish from the communicable public concept only by a process of abstraction. Whenever we deal with a concept we must have some particular presentation of it, *through* which we grasp it. (Langer 1979, 71–72; italics in the original)

FRENCH PERSPECTIVES

As noted earlier, Claude Lévi-Strauss, the preeminent French anthropologist in the study of symbols, was greatly influenced by the work of linguists in analyzing the way meaning is encoded in language. Lévi-Strauss considered myths to be culturally specific representations of universal human experiences and ways of thinking.

The British anthropologist Edmund Leach first advocated Lévi-Strauss's approach to analyzing myths, then later came to refute it. Leach and others have noted that the elements of a myth isolated by Lévi-Strauss can be arbitrary. Leach writes that Lévi-Strauss "first assumes that the myth (any myth) can readily be broken up into segments or incidents, and that everyone familiar with the story will agree as to what these incidents are" (1974, 67). Leach identifies two issues important to the study of symbols: (1) The meaning of symbols is arbitrary (culturally assigned), and (2) the interpretation of symbols is a subjective process.

SYMBOLS AND SOCIETY

The work of French anthropologists other than Lévi-Strauss also figures into the anthropological study of symbols. The most widely published French anthropologists view symbols as part of a dialectical process of social negotiation based on conceptual models. In his 1977 book *Discipline and Punish*, Michel Foucault notes that systems for punishing crimes are derived from ways of thinking about the nature of human society. Foucault describes the system of torture practiced by the French *ancien régime* before the Enlightenment as a drama acting out the "triumph of royal order over felons chosen for their symbolic value" (quoted in Certeau 1984, 45). Thus, models of punishment reflected the class system prevailing at the time. As a result of reforms carried out in the eighteenth century, the model of punishment changed to reflect the value of punishment equally applicable to all. Foucault's model suggests that the body politic imposes on the body of the felon a treatment incorporating a "body of doctrine."

Pierre Bourdieu (1972) extends to kinship systems the social model as a context for symbolic usage. In analyzing kinship practices, Bourdieu views them as "strategies" that organize concepts relating to fertility, inheritance, knowledge, hygiene, marriage, and economic and social investment, rather than as institutions that determine behavior. Though kinship strategies grow out of a symbolic system that defines the order of kin relations, actual practices may conflict with assumptions about the social order encoded in the symbolic system. The conflict between cultural assumptions and actual behavior is disguised in rituals that provide a "euphemism" for resolving the contradiction.

Though Bourdieu does not use this example, attitudes about marriage prevalent in the United States illustrate the interrelationship of symbolism, actual practice, and the reconciliation of cultural assumptions and actual behavior. In the United States, marriage is portrayed idealistically as the natural product of a romantic love relationship between a man and a woman. In actual practice, in the United States as elsewhere, marriage is a socially sanctioned institution that provides the economic framework for production and socialization of children.

The American marriage ritual and customs associated with marriage emphasize the romantic aspect of marriage while hinting at the pragmatic concerns that arise in marriage. As the ritual begins, the bride, wearing a white dress and carrying flowers, symbolizing both her sexual inexperience and her fertility, proceeds down the center aisle on her father's arm. Her path down the aisle links the families of bride and groom together, just as her fertility will later link them together as corelatives. Her father gives her hand to the groom at the foot of the altar, symbolically transferring her fertility from his own lineage to that of her husband-to-be. Though the surface emphasis is on the pair-bond created by the wedding ritual, it is generally understood that the romantic relationship between the bride and groom is less important to the social group than the newly created economic unit and generative family.

SOCIAL SPACE AND SYMBOLIC STRATEGY

Michel de Certeau analyzes popular culture—in which he includes folktales, mass media, and the use of consumer goods—as a means of defining one's social, physical, and conceptual space. Certeau suggests that "the practitioners of urban space" use language and other resources available to them to construct a particular type of reality.

> Thus a North African living in Paris or Roubaix [France] insinuates *into* the system imposed on him by the construction of a low-income housing development or of the French language the ways of "dwelling" (in a house or language) peculiar to his native Kabylia.... Without leaving the place where he has no choice but to live and which lays down its law for him, he establishes within it a degree of *plurality* and creativity. By an art of being in between, he draws unexpected results from his situation. (Certeau 1984, 30; italics in the original)

Beginning with Lévi-Strauss, the French approach has been aimed at uncovering the "logic" of assumptions underlying social behavior, whereas British social anthropologists have focused on analyzing social organization, which is presumed to provide the model for behavior. Except for Bronislaw Malinowski, British anthropologists have tended to reify social organization, analyzing it as a reality independent of individual actors, whereas contemporary French theorists emphasize the idea of social behavior as a cultural construct that is subject to continual renegotiation.

SEMIOTICS—CULTURE AS TEXT

The French view of the social order as a cultural construct has its counterpart in American anthropology, especially in studies influenced by the work of Clifford Geertz. It is not entirely accurate to classify Geertz as a semioticist, though he has defined his approach to culture as "essentially a semiotic one."

> Believing, with [the German sociologist and economist] Max Weber, that man is an animal suspended in webs of significance he himself has spun, I take culture to be those webs, and the analysis of it to be therefore not an experimental science in search of law but an interpretive one in search of meaning. (Geertz 1973, 5)

It would be difficult to classify Geertz in one-word categories. He is a seminal thinker who has greatly contributed to a range of anthropological studies. Publication of Geertz's 1973 book *The Interpretation of Cultures* stimulated a conceptual shift among many North American anthropologists. In a chapter of that book called "Thick Description: Toward an Interpretive Theory of Culture," Geertz asserts that, not only is human behavior essentially a social discourse that is culturally constructed, but the doing of ethnography is culturally constructed. "The ethnographer 'inscribes' social discourse; *he writes it down.* In so doing, he turns it from a passing event, which exists only in its own moment of occurrence, into an account, which exists in its inscriptions and can be reconsulted" (Geertz 1973, 19; italics in the original).

The implication is that the act of writing something down reifies an event or relationship that may be essentially ephemeral. It also means that reconsulting an ethnographic account can result in reinterpretation. Thus, the process of analysis is also culturally constructed. In his book *Works and Lives: The Anthropologist as Author*, Geertz insists that the process of writing anthropology is as important as formulating theory or choosing a method. In constructing an ethnography, Geertz notes, the anthropologist must convince people who have never been among the people being described that the people and events being described are authentic.

The ability of anthropologists to get us to take what they say seriously has less to do with either a factual look or an air of conceptual elegance than it has with their capacity to convince us that what they say is a result of their having actually penetrated (or if you prefer, been penetrated by) another form of life, of having, one way or another, truly "been there." And that, persuading us that this offstage miracle has occurred, is where the writing comes in. (Geertz 1988, 4–5)

The term "semiotics" derives from a philosophical approach to the study of signs and symbols that attempts to interpret their meaning according to their "grammar." In the anthropological case, semiotic studies focus on the way signs and symbols encode meaning according to rules of syntax and grammar, as well as on their relationship to the people who use them: "The culture of a people is an ensemble of texts, themselves ensembles, which the anthropologist strains to read over the shoulders of those to whom they properly belong" (Geertz 1971, 29). Geertz uses the term *semiotics* in the general sense of looking for meanings inherent in human interactions, as indicated by his description of interpretive anthropology: "The whole point of a semiotic approach to culture is . . . to aid us in gaining access to the conceptual world in which our subjects live so that we can, in some extended sense of the term, converse with them" (1973, 24).

According to Geertz, all human social life is based on the meaning it has for its participants. He notes, however, that "meanings can only be 'stored' in symbols: a cross, a crescent, or a feathered serpent." In other words, "Such religious symbols, dramatized in rituals or related in myths, are felt somehow to sum up, for those for whom they are resonant, what is known about the way the world is, the quality of the emotional life it supports, and the way one ought to behave while in it" (1973, 127).

Geertz illustrates the value of this type of interpretive anthropology in his landmark work "Deep Play: Notes on the Balinese Cockfight." In it, Geertz uses the cockfight as a means of gaining insight into an aspect of Balinese character not observable in other forms of social interaction.

What the cockfight says it says in a vocabulary of sentiment—the thrill of risk, the despair of loss, the pleasure of triumph. Yet what it says is not merely that risk is exciting, loss depressing, or triumph gratifying, banal tautologies of affect, but that it is of these emotions, thus exampled, that society is built and individuals put together. (Geertz 1971, 27)

Geertz's seminal work on interpretive anthropology has spun off a branch of semiotic analysis that attempts to analyze symbolic systems and cultural interactions by applying linguistic principles aimed at uncovering the underlying meaning of the interaction. In fact, all cultural exchanges involve multiple levels of meanings, as Geertz asserts, all of them "true" insofar as they explain what it means to be human, both for members of a particular culture and for the anthropologist attempting to understand it.

MATERIALISM VERSUS IDEALISM

There has long been a debate in some anthropological circles over whether behavior and worldview are caused by pragmatic considerations or whether ideas cause behavior. The former is known as the materialist position; the latter is known as the idealist position. As is the case with many such oppositional views, the answer lies somewhere in between.

THE MATERIALIST PERSPECTIVE

The materialist perspective has been greatly influenced by Karl Marx and his collaborator, Friedrich Engels. According to Marx, sociocultural life is organized into two main parts: the economic infrastructure, or base, and the superstructure. The superstructure is further divided into the legal-political arrangements, which include kinship and political systems, and the social consciousness, or ideology. Marx saw the relationship among these components as a dialectic resulting from conflicts between social classes seeking to gain control over the economic base.

According to the Marxist model, the purpose of ideology is to justify social behavior, which in reality is based in competition for control over economic resources. Religion is part of the ideological system that justifies control over the means of production, or as Marx put it, "Religion . . . is the opium of the people."[3]

As framed by Marvin Harris, the materialist perspective "is based on the simple premise that human social life is a response to the practical problems of earthly existence" (1979, ix). In application, the materialist approach asserts that the driving force underlying human behavior is the need to produce and allocate material resources, or in more general terms, to adapt energy for human use.

> We have been taught to value elaborate "spiritualized" explanations of cultural phenomena more than down-to-earth material ones. I contend

that the solution to [apparent cultural riddles such as the Hindu sacred cow and the Kwakiutl potlatch] lies in a better understanding of practical circumstances. I shall show that even the most bizarre-seeming beliefs and practices turn out on closer inspection to be based on ordinary, banal, one might say "vulgar" conditions, needs, and activities. (Harris 1974, 2–3)

The "ordinary," "banal," and "vulgar" conditions identified by Harris as the motivating force underlying behavior are material concerns. In the case of the Hindu ban on killing cows, Harris argues that in India cattle are more productive alive than dead since living cows provide milk for consumption, dung for fuel, and traction for plowing. Once they die, cattle provide an economic resource for members of the outcaste, who alone are able to process the hide and other byproducts and who sell the meat to non-Hindus. Raising cattle purely to obtain beef, Harris argues, is a luxury that Hindus cannot afford, though it is commonplace in the United States.

Because of the high level of beef consumption in the United States, three-quarters of all our croplands are used for feeding cattle rather than people. Since the per capita calorie intake in India is already below minimum daily requirements, switching croplands to meat production could only result in higher food prices and a further deterioration in the living standards for poor families. I doubt if more than 10 percent of the Indian people will ever be able to make beef an important part of their diet, regardless of whether they believe in cow love or not. (Harris 1974, 17)

THE IDEALIST PERSPECTIVE

A perspective that Harris would define as idealist is framed by Harold Courlander in his 1971 book *The Fourth World of the Hopis.* For about two thousand years or more, before the appropriation of much of their land by European colonialists, the Hopis practiced a form of shifting horticulture based on cultivation of maize (corn). Modern Hopi territory centers on the Black Mesa area east of the Grand Canyon, in what is now Arizona. The emergence of Hopis into what they describe as the Fourth World, their travels through the region, and the division of the Hopis into clans is recounted in a series of myths.

It is generally assumed that what motivated these population movements was the endless search for surroundings that would provide for elemental human physical needs. But if surviving myths and legends are listened to with care they may tell us that these restless ancestors were also searching for places of spiritual harmony with nature. For throughout the myths and myth-legends are references to flights from imperfection and evil, and to long journeys in fulfillment of moral prophecy. (Courlander 1971, 9–10)

Courlander is asserting that the emic (insider) explanation—the Hopi concept of their travel as flights from imperfection and evil undertaken in fulfillment of a moral prophecy—is more "true" than the etic (outsider) perspective taken by cultural materialists that the travels were undertaken for economic reasons.

RECONCILING MATERIALISM WITH IDEALISM

In fact, there is no contradiction between the need to provide for "elemental human physical needs" on the one hand and "flights from imperfection and evil" or journeys undertaken "in fulfillment of moral prophecy" on the other. Throughout the world, travels are explained by the people involved as having been undertaken at the behest of the gods or an all-powerful God.

In their two-hundred-year journey from Aztlan to the Valley of Mexico, the Mexica, or Aztecs, ritually consulted their divinity, Huizilopochtli, a war god associated with the sun, and followed his council regarding their travels. In one case described by the sixteenth-century Spanish chronicler Diego Durán (1964, 18–21), Mexica who opposed the will of Huitzilopochtli and refused to continue their travels were sacrificed to the god under the cover of night. Frances F. Berdan analyzes that practice in terms of the dynamics of the group: "The wrath of Huitzilopochtli was expressed, and the rebellious faction was eliminated" (1982, 5). It might also be noted that the authority of the priests who interpreted and carried out the will of Huitzilopochtli was reinforced through the sacrifice. Thus, serving Huitzilopochtli reinforced the authority of the priesthood, maintained the solidarity of the group, eliminated dissent, and facilitated the travels of the Mexica into the Valley of Mexico.

Similarly, in leading the Israelites out of Egypt, as chronicled in the Biblical book of Exodus, Moses was told by G-d that He would lead the people to "a land flowing with milk and honey" (Exodus 3:8). The journey out of Egypt was attended by a series of wonders, including the parting of the Red Sea, Moses's vision of a burning bush, the gift of food miraculously supplied by heaven, and a contract between G-d and humans in the form of the Ten Commandments. Thus, the pragmatic necessity of escaping bondage during a time of tribulation is reinforced symbolically by "evidence" that the journey is divinely ordained.

The emic, symbolic view of the flight of Israelites from Egypt is no more or less "true" than the etic, anthropological view. The symbolic view focuses on the meaning of the events for the participants; the analytical view focuses on the structural or economic impetus for the flight.

Conceptually, there is no clear binary division between materialist and idealist explanations. Neither Emile Durkheim nor Bronislaw Malinowski nor a number of other anthropologists dismissed by Harris as idealist would assert that ideas alone drive human behavior. Malinowski asserted that social organization serves human biological and psychological needs. Durkheim did not deal directly with the role of material culture but instead focused on the relationship of social organization to the way in which humans conceptualize their universe. Most of the social scientists Harris criticizes for not attending to material aspects of culture were focusing on a different aspect of the human experience: how humans articulate their relationship to each other and how they conceptualize their experience of the world.

Regardless of how holistic anthropologists try to be in describing the lives of the people they study, ethnography is ultimately an inexact process, and much depends on the life experiences of the ethnographer. Renato Rosaldo illustrates this point in his essay "Grief and a Headhunter's Rage." When Rosaldo asked an Ilongot man of northern Luzon, Philippines, why men of his generation took heads, the anthropologist was told that "rage, born of grief, impels him to kill his fellow human beings. . . . The act of severing and tossing away the victim's head enables him, he says, to vent and, he hopes, throw away the anger of his bereavement" (1989, 1).

Rosaldo considered this explanation "too simple, thin, opaque, implausible, stereotypical, or otherwise unsatisfying." He tells us, "Probably I naïvely equated grief with sadness. Certainly no personal experience allowed me to imagine the powerful rage Ilongots claimed to find in bereavement" (1989, 3). Rosaldo drew on the anthropological theoretical construct of exchange theory to develop the idea that headhunting resulted from the way that one death canceled out the other.

Fourteen years later, Rosaldo discovered that the Ilongot emic description of headhunting explained an aspect of grief more accurately than his etic anthropological analysis. While conducting research among the Ifugaos of northern Luzon, Philippines, his wife, Michelle Zimbalist Rosaldo, "lost her footing and fell to her death some 65 feet down a sheer precipice into a swollen river below." Rosaldo tells us, "Immediately on finding her body, I became enraged. How could she abandon me? How could she have been so stupid as to fall? I tried to cry. I sobbed, but rage blocked the tears" (1989, 9). Rosaldo learned that grief cannot be reduced to anger, but anger is a part of the complex emotions that make up grief.

> Powerful visceral emotional states swept over me, at times separately and at other times together. I experienced the deep cutting pain of sorrow almost beyond endurance, the cadaverous cold of realizing the finality of death, the trembling beginning in my abdomen and spreading through my body, the mournful keening that started without my willing, and frequent tearful sobbing. (1989, 9)

Ultimately, Rosaldo's own powerful experience led him to understand the process of grieving that underlay the Ilongot practice of headhunting (now outlawed).

> Ilongot anger and my own overlap, rather like two circles, partially overlaid and partially separate. They are not identical. . . . My vivid fantasies, for example, about a life insurance agent who refused to recognize Michelle's death as job-related did not lead me to kill him, cut off his head, and celebrate afterward. (1989, 10)

Instead, Rosaldo drew on an anthropological means of dealing with grief through catharsis. He channeled his hard-won insights into the emic perspective on grief by writing "Grief and a Headhunter's Rage."

Harris is correct in pointing out that explanations of human behavior often leave pragmatic concerns out of the picture. Human life could not continue without food, water, and other material necessities, and the importance of these resources means they must surely have an impact on symbolic forms. At the same time, symbols shape the way people view their environment, which, equally certainly, must have an impact on the way they utilize material resources. In fact, food, water, the earth, the sun, bears, fish, sheep, cows, and other environmental resources are found in symbolic systems throughout the world. The availability of these resources, in fact, often plays a central role in the symbolic systems of particular cultures. The importance of material concerns is powerfully expressed in the Twenty-Third Psalm of the Bible:

The Lord is my shepherd; I shall not want.
He maketh me to lie down in green pastures: he leadeth me beside the still waters.

He restoreth my soul; he leadeth me in the paths of righteousness for his name's sake.

Yea, though I walk through the valley of the shadow of death, I will fear no evil; for thou art with me; thy rod and thy staff they comfort me.

Thou preparest a table before me in the presence of mine enemies: thou anointest my head with oil; my cup runneth over.

Surely goodness and mercy shall follow me all the days of my life: and I will dwell in the house of the Lord for ever.

This poem expresses the relationship of humans to the divine in symbolic terms as the relationship between sheep and their shepherd. In doing so, it does not leave pragmatic concerns out of the picture. In fact, it enumerates the requirements for human survival in an often uncertain and dangerous world.

SYMBOLIC ECOLOGY

The complementary relationship between emic views (often expressed symbolically) and etic views (as reflected in anthropological analyses) is explicitly reconciled in a redefined symbolic ecology. The path for this approach was paved by Roy Rappaport in his book *Pigs for the Ancestors*, published in 1968. Rappaport theorized that *kaiko*, ritual pig sacrifices to the ancestors among the Tsembaga Waring of New Guinea, regulate relationships both within a group and between groups. In addition, the slaughter of pigs preserves the ecological balance of the group to its environment by preventing the development of large pig populations.

Claims to subterritories within Tsembaga territory are asserted and affirmed symbolically by ritually planting cordyline bushes that mark the territory of a particular clan. The bushes are called *yu miñ rumbim*. Yu miñ refers to men's souls; rumbim is the Tsembaga name for the cordyline. "Every adult male member of the subterritorial group participates in this ritual by grasping the *rumbim* as it is planted, thus symbolizing both his connection to the land and his membership in the group that claims the land" (Rappaport 1968, 19).

The cordyline ritual defines gardening territories for each of the three Tsembaga groups, thus reducing disputes over competing claims and distributing the Tsembaga over a broad area that does not overtax their environment. Rituals relating to planting and uprooting the cordyline, as well as rituals associated with preparing for the pig sacrifice, provide the means of defining relationships within and between groups. In addition, warfare is held in abeyance until debts to allies and ancestors are paid in the preparations for and conduct of the kaiko ceremony. Thus, debts—and any grievances associated with them—are resolved in the preparations for the kaiko ceremony.

Rappaport distinguished between "cognized" and "operational" models: "The cognized model is the model of the environment conceived by the people who act in it" (1968, 238). "The operational model is that which the anthropologist constructs through observation and measurement of empirical entities, events, and material relationships" (237). The difference between cognized models and operational models loosely corresponds to the distinction between emic and etic perspectives. Rappaport viewed the operational model constructed by the anthropologist as the "true" model.

Rappaport's error consisted of assuming there is only one "true" explanation for human behavior. Whether emic or etic, models never hold an exclusive franchise on "truth." Just as a map is a simplified schema of geographical terrain, models of social relationships are simplified models of sociocultural terrain. Both forms of terrain are far too complex to be reduced to a single map or model.

Aletta Biersack (1999a) identifies three branches of the newer ecological approach: symbolic ecology, historical ecology, and political ecology. Biersack rejects older cultural ecology models, which "reduced culture to nature by explaining particular symbolic and behavioral repertoires as adaptive tools" that promoted survival in a particular environment (1999b, 71). This is "reductionist," Biersack says, because the environment is "transformed by human action" (1999b, 71). Her approach to analyzing the relationship of humans to the environment is a dialectical one that centers on the emic perspective—Rappaport's cognized models or Geertz's "local knowledge" (1983)—"as the framework for and motivation of human activity, at the heart of its analysis" (1999b, 71).

Biersack provides an example of the new symbolic ecology as an explanatory model in her article "The Mount Kare Python and His Gold: Totemism and Ecology in the Papua New Guinea Highlands" (1999b). Central to this analysis are emic beliefs about a giant python, Taiyundika, whose bones lie at the bottom of the lake bearing his name. The python is a totemic ancestor to the clans of the people who occupy the area around Mount Kare. According to legend, the python was killed through the machinations of one of his daughters. Traditionally, the people of the region ceremonially dropped pork into the lake as a sacrifice to the python.

The ancestral python is a symbol of regeneration and fertility. People of the region have observed that snakes in general regenerate themselves by shedding their skins. In addition, the ancestral python left descendants as evidenced today in the lives of the people of the region. "The landscape is strewn with [the python's] remains, his bones and blood. In sacrificing pigs to the ancestor, the python's living descendants assure the health and fertility of this same landscape, viewed as a plenum of human, animal, and plant species—clans and their totems" (Biersack 1996b, 74).

With the discovery of gold at Mount Kare in 1988, beliefs about fertility and regeneration relating to the python were adapted to the new conditions. The people viewed the gold as a gift from the ancestors arising from the body of the python itself. Biersack explains the symbolic link that establishes continuity between the people's experience of the environment before and after the discovery of gold. "As a totemic figure, the Mt. Kare python is ancestral to the clans of the region. Today he is also ancestral to the gold, which is mythologized as his flesh" (1999b, 71).

Thus, the ancestral symbol leads the way to the utilization and distribution of resources that have contemporary value.

THE ECLECTIC APPROACH

Earlier in this book, I asserted that people will die for a symbol. Anthropologists can become almost equally passionate in defending their particular approaches to the study of symbols, though there has yet to be actual blood shed on the subject in the halls of academia. Anthropologists defend their territory on the subject of symbols with much the same vehemence that gang members defend their 'hoods. In some cases, anthropological debates about symbols are semantic, based on how the anthropologists involved define the concept of symbol. In other cases, there can be real disagreements about the nature of symbols and their role in the organization of human groups or in the psychology of human beings.

As is the case with many other anthropologists, my own approach to the study of symbols is eclectic. The eclectic approach allows the anthropologist to examine the use of symbols in a variety of contexts. Since the eclectic approach is data driven rather than defined by a particular theoretical perspective, it allows the researcher to integrate data from a variety of sources, as illustrated by my studies of symbols in a number of contexts.

My interest in the social, conceptual, and psychological dynamics of symbols was sparked by my study of healing rituals in a Spiritualist group in

South Central Los Angeles. Spiritualist belief and practices are organized around the idea that spirits of the dead can be contacted for the purpose of healing, solving day-to-day problems, and learning about "life on the other side," that is, after death.

My initial models for examining this aspect of Spiritualist belief and practice combined Festinger, Riecken, and Schachter's social psychological model (1956) and B. F. Skinner's behaviorist model (2002 [1971]) with Victor Turner's social anthropological approach. Following Festinger's and Skinner's models, I suggested that Spiritualist healing rituals promote commitment to the group by requiring "patients" to demonstrate their faith before the entire congregation. Patients publicly demonstrated their faith by acting out a drama of illness and healing that was rewarded by the approval of the group (Womack 1978).

I drew on Turner's analysis of male puberty rituals and healing practices among the Ndembu to explain the role of ritual in articulating social relationships within the group. Turner found that "the Ndembu 'doctor' sees his task less as curing an individual than as remedying the ills of a corporate group. The sickness of a patient is mainly a sign that 'something is rotten' in the corporate body" (1967, 392). Similarly, among the Spiritualists, healing and other rituals that involved contacting the spirits reflected an association between the health of the individual and the solidarity of the group as a whole (Womack 1977).

My research in the group took quite another turn when I became an observer of the transfer of power from what the sociologist Max Weber (1973) calls a "charismatic leader" to an elected leader. In witnessing the transition of leadership from a prophet, whose power is based on personal revelation or charisma, to a priest, whose power is based on the authority of a hierarchical office, I was able to study the emergence of factions and the contesting of "legitimate" forms of leadership. These behaviors were observable both in actual behavior of members of the group as they jockeyed for position in the new order and in their contesting by interpreting the symbolic forms of myth and ritual.

SYMBOLS AND ACTION

My intriguing look into the multiple levels of symbols—acted out in the psychological drama of healing and the social drama of contested leadership in the Spiritualist church—led me to seek an arena in which to test competing theories about whether ritual is based primarily in psychological or in social processes. Anthropologists had long noted that ritual is closely associated with risk and anxiety (e.g., Malinowski 1927; 1954) but have debated whether the thrust of ritual is psychological or social. I addressed this issue by conducting a long-term study of the relationship of risk and use of ritual by professional athletes.

Athletes are symbolic actors par excellence. They act as adepts in conducting their own rituals of preparation and protection. They also serve as heroic warriors in symbolic dramas staged for society as a whole. I determined that both psychological and social factors play significant roles in sports ritual and that, for this group, risks associated with winning and losing are more significant factors than physical danger. I also noted that physical danger and group solidarity are more significant factors in rituals of hockey and football players than in rituals of baseball players and that this is related to the degree of danger and style of play in the three sports (Womack 1982). I also suggested that rituals enhance performance by allowing an athlete to "screen out distractions and order his world so that he is free to concentrate on the game" (Womack 1992, 300).

After completing my study of rituals of professional athletes, I became interested in the role of sports as a symbolic drama enacting and resolving social conflicts, an issue of ongoing interest in the study of athletic contests. As this aspect of my research developed, I conducted a cross-cultural study of the portrayal of athletes in various forms of expressive culture, including art, literature, and music, in an attempt to determine whether consistent or universal themes exist in sports. In addition to anthropologists such as John Roberts and Brian Sutton-Smith (1966), scholars in the fields of philosophy, history, and sociology have long debated this issue. My findings support the idea that sports act out universal themes of contesting but that the symbolic expression of these themes is particular to the social context. For example, hunting is a pervasive theme in sporting art and literature, but the symbolic messages that hunting conveys vary depending on the social and cultural context. Hunting by royals in stratified societies in China, the ancient Middle East, and Europe emphasizes royal prerogative and privilege. In other societies, hunting art and literature emphasize an equal contest between the hunter and the hunted, as in William Faulkner's short story "The Bear." In still other cases, the hunt symbolizes an erotic chase, as in Ovid's treatise *The Art of Love* and "Huntsman, What Quarry?" Edna St. Vincent Millay's poem (see Womack 2003).

The eclectic approach greatly aided my analysis of the art and literature of sporting traditions as varied as the Central American ball game, American Indian foot races, and the aristocratic hunting traditions of Europe, Egypt, ancient Persia, and ancient China, among others. In this case, I augmented my essentially social anthropological approach with input from other anthropological models. For example, I drew on Lévi-Strauss's structuralist model as an aid in analyzing sports symbolism in Greek myths and on the cultural materialist model in analyzing hunting traditions in ancient Egypt and Persia. My survey of sporting art and literature convinced me of the value of incorporating multiple models in analyzing symbols.

LEARNING ABOUT SYMBOLS

Overall, four general trends have emerged in the anthropological study of symbols:

1. Approaches to symbols based on dynamic or dialectic schema—emphasizing symbolizing as process rather than product—are displacing deterministic models that treat symbols as static.
2. The linear quest for a "primal cause" or single external verifiable force that "causes" symbols is being replaced by a recognition that use of symbols is shaped in a multidimensional context.
3. Symbolic systems are now viewed as cognitive maps that do not operate primarily on either the psychological or the social level. Instead, they organize the human experience within a particular social and cultural context shaped by a variety of forces, including the environment and concepts about the body and human nature, as well as the organization of power, work, allocation of material goods, and kinship relations.
4. Cognitive or symbolic maps are not based in erroneous thinking resulting from ignorance about the "real" causes of things but are models for organizing human experience according to the meaning it holds for members of a particular group.

The approach presented in *Symbols and Meaning* is an eclectic one, partly because the book is intended to reflect a variety of anthropological approaches to the study of symbols rather than a partisan defense of one particular approach. In addition, it is my position that all approaches to symbolic analysis have their merits. In the Biblical story of Genesis, for example, G-d or Yahweh created the world by establishing a series of binary oppositions—light is divided from darkness, the firmament is made distinct from the waters, and Heaven is separated from Earth—thus supporting

Lévi-Strauss's model of mythological organization. In addition, the Creator defined relationships among various aspects of the creation—including the relationship of humans to animals, of humans to G-d, and of men and women to each other—thus supporting the Durkheimian model. All creation myths, and symbolic systems in general, defy simple, unilinear, causal analysis.

In my anthropology courses, I ask students to analyze the story of Little Red Ridinghood using first the Freudian model, then the Lévi-Straussian model, then the social model developed by Victor Turner. In the course of the assignment, it becomes clear that Little Red Ridinghood is a cautionary tale, though use of a particular analytical model shapes the interpretation of what the child is being cautioned against.

Freudian analysis suggests that the child is being instructed in the dangers of inappropriate sex. Lévi-Strauss's approach indicates that the tale cautions against mixing of conceptual categories organized around the binary opposition of the wild and the tame. The mixing of categories is resolved when the tame woodsman emerges from the wild forest and kills the wild wolf who has invaded the tame grandmother's house, the entire episode having been instigated by Little Red Ridinghood's invasion of the wild by straying from the tame path. According to Victor Turner's model, the story is a means of instructing a child in the organization of social relationships and the importance of conforming to cultural norms.

The eclectic approach would assert that all these interpretations have merit and that all are potentially correct. The analyst would then look for other indications in the social and cultural context to evaluate which of the approaches would best explain this particular case. Since symbols are multivocal, conveying multiple levels of meaning, the child listening to the story is likely to hear many messages at the same time.

NOTES

1. Malinowski is not alone in noting that symbolic thought and pragmatic thought can coexist. In his book *Witchcraft, Oracles, and Magic among the Azande*, E. E. Evans-Pritchard noted that he participated in Zande oracle procedures: "I always kept a supply of poison for the use of my household and neighbours and we regulated our affairs in accordance with the oracles' decision. I may remark that I found this as satisfactory a way of running my home and affairs as any other" (1976, 126).

2. From "Dirge without Music," *Collected Lyrics of Edna St. Vincent Millay* (New York: Harper and Row, 1917).

3. From the introduction to Marx's *Critique of the Hegelian Philosophy of Right*, published in 1844.

3

SYMBOLS AND
SOCIAL ORGANIZATION

The importance of symbolic forms—including religion, magic, and expressive culture—in defining and articulating the dynamics of social life has long been recognized. The French sociologist Emile Durkheim (1915) suggested that religion is social organization projected into the heavens. At the time of Durkheim's writing, the prevailing view was that religion was a form of "primitive science" that would disappear as soon as science found answers to all the questions involved in understanding the universe. The prevailing view of nineteenth-century scholars was that "primitive humans" invented religion to explain what were to them seemingly incomprehensible natural phenomena: Why are there eclipses of the sun and moon? What is lightning?

Durkheim pointed out that nature is, on the whole, predictable. It would be surprising if the sun *didn't* come up in the morning. In general, humans can count on nature to do what it is supposed to do. On the other hand, human beings can be unpredictable and inexplicable. The most incomprehensible factor governing human life, Durkheim noted, is society, the invisible and powerful force of collective action.

Humans are social animals. As infants, we could not survive in the absence of virtually constant care from other humans. Most of human brain development takes place after birth, during a time when we are almost constantly interacting with others. The anthropologist Clifford Geertz (1973) called human beings "the incomplete animal" because most of human development begins at birth, when the infant is dropped kicking and screaming into its social world.

From the time we are born, our behavior is shaped by the expectations of others. Restrictions and permissions are imposed on us in a seemingly arbitrary way. The psychologist Sigmund Freud observed, "An infant at the breast does not as yet distinguish his ego from the external world as the source of the sensations flowing in upon him. He gradually learns to do so, in response to various promptings" (1961, 13–14).

Throughout our lives we interact with other people according to a design that often coerces us to act against our own self-interest. Why is it, for example, that older men can coerce younger men into fighting a war that may take them away from their wives and prevent them from living to see their children grow up? Why is it that Queen Elizabeth can control much of England's wealth while performing almost none of its labor? Why is it that rulers of stratified societies have the power of life and death over their subjects? Why do people deem it necessary to perform rituals for their ancestors? Durkheim suggested that religions encode answers to these kinds of questions in ways that promote the solidarity of the group.

Conversely, the social organization of a particular group helps to shape the world view of the people in it and the types of symbols it produces. In this chapter, we will consider the relationship of symbols to the organization of power in a group, to the production and distribution of material resources, and to the organization of kinship. We will also discuss the role of symbols in social control and in defining social boundaries.

POLITICS, POWER, AND SYMBOLS

Political systems organize relationships of power within a group. In terms of symbols, the most important aspect of political organization is whether the group is *egalitarian* or *hierarchical* (stratified). In egalitarian societies, there is relatively little social differentiation and relatively equal access to power and resources. Task specialization takes place only along lines of age and gender: all adult males perform the same tasks and all adult females perform the same tasks. Almost all members of the group are likely to be involved in food production or will make other economic contributions. Children and elders perform tasks appropriate to their perceived abilities.

In an egalitarian society, no one has absolute power over any other. The ability to influence others is based on an individual's personal characteristics, such as the ability to hunt, to heal people, to build alliances, to perform music, or to tell stories.

In hierarchical societies, power is vested in a particular social role or office. There is a great deal of task specialization and unequal access to power and resources. A group's being able to coerce others into fighting a war that benefits mainly the group, controlling most of a nation's wealth while doing very little of its work, and having the power of life and death over others are characteristics of a hierarchical society. Performing rituals for our ancestors is characteristic of all human groups.

The models of power and influence, on which anthropological models of political organization are based, were developed by Max Weber (1947) and Talcott Parsons (1963). Weber defined *power* as the ability to carry out one's will in spite of the opposition of others. Parsons identified persuasion as the basis of *influence*. An individual can influence others by persuading them that it is in their best interest to behave as one wishes them to. The allocation of power and the ability to use influence in a society are expressed in its symbolic system in two ways: (1) the perceived relationship of humans to spirit beings and (2) the ability of humans to control and use symbols.

GODS, SPIRIT BEINGS, AND SOCIAL GROUPS

Durkheim based his model of the relationship of religion to society on his analysis of totems among Australian Aborigines, who trace their origins to a totemic ancestor, typically conceived of as an animal. The clan, a kin group whose members trace descent from this ancestor, takes its name from the totemic animal. The totemic animal is represented symbolically in all ceremonies, in the landscape, and in taboos and rituals. Durkheim writes, "The totem is before all a symbol, a material expression of something else" (1915, 236). He adds, "In the first place, it is the outward and visible form of . . . the totemic principle or god. But it is also the symbol of the determined society called the clan" (1915, 236).

Durkheim compares the totem to a flag, a visible mark that distinguishes one group from another and permeates all aspects of the social life of clan members. He then asserts that the "god" and the clan are the same entity: "The god of the clan, the totemic principle, can therefore be nothing else than the clan itself, personified and represented to the imagination under the visible form of the animal or vegetable which serves as a totem" (1915, 236).

Because it is personified and made visible, the totemic symbol coerces members of a group to engage in behavior believed to please an entity on whom they think they depend. In other words, the totem or god *is society*: "It is because of this that at every instant we are obliged to submit ourselves to rules of conduct and thought which we have neither made nor desired, and which are sometimes even contrary to our most fundamental inclinations and instincts" (1915, 237).

In his book *The Birth of the Gods*, the sociologist Guy Swanson (1966) built on Durkheim's model, aiming to more precisely define the relationship between social organization and beliefs in particular types of spirit beings or forces. Swanson considered the following attributes to be important in shaping views of the supernatural: (1) the presence of what he calls sovereign organizations within the society and (2) the degree of complexity, specialization, and wealth of a society. Both attributes may be described in anthropological terms as relating to the degree of stratification in a society. Using these criteria, Swanson surveyed fifty societies on which sufficient data were available from the ethnographic literature compiled by anthropologists.

Swanson discovered that belief in a "high god," a creator god or god having ultimate control of the universe, is strongly correlated with the presence of three or more sovereign groups within a society.

> Such a god is rarely found. Even in the highly developed monotheism of Judaism and Christianity, God shares the supernatural world with demons, angels, Satan, and such honored dead as the saints. True, He created this cloud of beings, but they have an existence of their own and exhibit distinctive purposes. (Swanson 1966, 55)

Swanson then turned his attention to polytheism, belief in a number of superior gods. Typically, Swanson notes, these superior gods are specialized, with authority over a specific area or craft. In the case of Greek and Roman gods, Poseidon was lord of the sea, Demeter ruled the agricultural cycle and agricultural production, Diana aided women in childbirth and governed the forests. All wild plants and animals also fell under her jurisdiction (Swanson 1966, 83).

Swanson correlated the number of superior gods to the number of what he called communal specialties in a society, which may be loosely defined as task specialization, though the resulting correlation was not as strong as in the case of high gods. Swanson then correlated a belief in the presence of ancestor spirits who are active in the affairs of human beings with the presence of sovereign kinship groups, kin groups that are larger than the nuclear family and that control a territory.

DIFFICULTIES IN COUNTING GODS

Swanson's efforts to subject the often unruly mélange of supernatural beings believed in cross-culturally to statistical analysis was ultimately more instructive than conclusive. Accurate descriptions of spirit beliefs are difficult to come by in the ethnographic literature because these beliefs tend to be vaguely defined even by the people who hold them. As I note in *Being Human: An Introduction to Cultural Anthropology*, "Beliefs about spirit beings vary considerably from one society to another, so that it is virtually impossible to sort into neat categories the vast array of spirit beings known to people throughout the world" (Womack 1998, 195).

In addition, as Swanson notes, ethnographers may not compile a comprehensive list of spirit beings, so that a belief in what he calls a "high god" may be present in a group but not reported by the anthropologist. "Shall we assume that such a deity may exist but not be reported by the anthropologist? I propose that, in most cases, we shall not go astray if we conclude that these villagers have no such deity" (Swanson 1966, 50). Swanson is making a reasonable assumption on the theoretical level, but it may be an untenable assumption on the methodological level. Statistical analyses rely on precise data collection techniques, and conceptual beings are not so easily counted as physical beings.

A further difficulty in Swanson's analysis is that his model is based solely on formal, public recognition of power, which may be subverted in private, informal ways. David D. Gilmore (1993) notes that the ability of women of Andalusia, in southern Spain, to control the private, domestic sphere counterbalances public models of men as being able to "rule." Similarly, Louise Lamphere (1974) and Margery Wolf (1974) found that women could influence public behavior through their control of domestic arrangements.

These findings are especially relevant to discussions of spirit beings because informal strategies for controlling the behavior of others are often acted out through negotiation of symbols, including spirit mediumship (Elliott 1955) and charges of devil possession (Crain 1993). Through spirit mediumship an individual lacking power in the public realm can exert a great deal of influence by interpreting the will of the spirits. Similarly, a low-status person can undercut the power of authorities through charges of devil possession or witchcraft.

Ultimately, the variables involved in analyzing spirit beings are far too complex to be enumerated precisely. As noted earlier, symbols bring together multiple levels of association, conceptual, social, experiential, and contextual, and the precise way in which these elements fit together cannot be readily identified, even by the person believing in or using the symbol.

HUMAN BEINGS AND SPIRIT BEINGS

In dealing with the relationship between power and symbols, it is instructive to turn once again to Durkheim, who notes that symbolic systems define the source of power. For Durkheim, power arises from social forces, the invisible power of social groups to compel, coerce, and shape the destinies of their members. Since the source of power in human groups is often difficult to isolate and define, and since the nature of spirit beings is rarely defined with precision, generalizations about the relationship between human beings and spirit beings must be approached with caution.

In general, as Swanson noted, spirit beings with absolute power are most likely to be found in hierarchical societies. This is because the concept of absolute power is derived from the experience of socially derived absolute authority. If a U.S. president can subvert my plans to attend college by inducting me into the armed forces, then God—who is even more powerful—also has power of life and death over me. In the Bible, King David had power of life and death over his subjects, a power that is found only in hierarchical societies. Similarly, the Judeo-Christian God is symbolically represented as having absolute power over human beings. The absolute power of God, and representations of that entity as male, reflect the authority of the male lineage head in a stratified patrilineal society. This relationship can be noted with some precision.

The !Kung of Africa's Kalahari Desert pose a different issue of analysis. The !Kung are a relatively egalitarian society that traditionally lived by foraging. In !Kung society, no man or woman had power over any other. Important decisions were made by consensus of the group, a process in which people discuss an issue until they arrive at agreement. Similarly, relations with beings in the spirit world are negotiated through persuasion. Marjorie Shostak has described the negotiation process in healing, in which the soul of the healer travels to the spirit world to discover the cause of the illness: "An ancestral spirit or a god is usually found responsible and asked to reconsider. If the healer is persuasive and the spirit agrees, the sick person recovers. If the spirit is elusive or unsympathetic, a cure is not achieved" (1981, 292–93).

Just as humans have relative degrees of power, beings in the spirit world are seen as having relative degrees of power. !Kung believe in "a major god in command of an entourage of lesser gods" (Shostak 1981, 291).

> The realm of the spiritual infuses all aspects of !Kung physical and social life, and is seen as a fundamental determinant in the delicate balance be-

tween life and death, sickness and health, rain and drought, abundance and scarcity. . . . Both the greater and lesser deities are modeled on humans, and their characteristics reflect the multitude of possibilities inherent in the human spirit. Sometimes they are kind, humane, and generous; at other times, whimsical, vindictive, or cruel. Their often erratic behavior is thought responsible for the unpredictability of human life and death. (Shostak 1981, 291)

Though the relationship between characteristics of human beings and spirit beings is clear from this example, it is more difficult to locate the social source of the "major god" who has the power to command other gods. Nisa, the !Kung woman whose life was chronicled by Shostak, describes the absolute power of God as controlling even the animals in the bush and the arrows of the hunter: "Even if the hunter had seen many animals, his arrows would never strike them. Because if God refuses to part with an animal, the man's arrows won't be able to kill it. . . . That is God's way; that is how God does things and how it is for us as we live. Because God controls everything" (1981, 300).

How did a relatively egalitarian group such as the !Kung, in which decisions are made by consensus, develop a symbolic image of a being with power to command? It may be that this aspect of !Kung belief can be traced to their interactions with more powerful outsiders. Edwin N. Wilmsen notes that San foragers, including the !Kung, "have been subjected to incursions from other groups for millennia" (2001, 264). Among these powerful outsiders are Bantu and Herero pastoralists and horticulturalists, European and American traders in ivory and ostrich feathers, and stratified Batswana people, who served as mediators between the European traders and Kalahari suppliers. The interactions of !Kung with these powerful outsiders—who must have seemed alternately "kind, humane, and generous" or "whimsical, vindictive, or cruel"—may have formed the basis for their view of a god having the power to command others.

Nisa's description of God suggests the influence of colonial powers: "God is the power that made people. He is like a person with a person's body and covered with beautiful clothes. He has a horse on which he puts people who are just learning to trance" (Shostak 1981, 300). Since horses are not indigenous to sub-Saharan groups, God's horsemanship suggests the influence of outsiders.

Even God—and perhaps colonial authority—is not immune to human persuasion, however. Nisa explains her ability to heal: "I am a master at trancing to drum-medicine songs. I lay hands on people and they usually get better. I know how to trick God from wanting to kill someone and how to have God give the person back to me" (Shostak 1981, 303).

SECULAR AND SACRED FORMS OF POWER

The organization of power in secular matters is reflected in the allocation of power in symbolic institutions, including religion, the arts, and forms of play. The organization of power in the Roman Catholic Church reflects the organization of power in a medieval monarchy, a social context within which the Church developed. At the head of the hierarchy is the Pope, whose authority is absolute. He is surrounded by the college of cardinals, which is equivalent to the monarch's court. As described by a Catholic source, "Cardinals are chosen by the Holy Father [the Pope] to serve as his principal assistants and advisers in the central administration of church affairs."[1] Ranking immediately below the cardinals are the archbishops, the regional administrators, who correspond to the local lords of medieval Europe. The archbishops preside over bishops, who preside in turn over parish priests, who preside over local districts.

Religious personnel in the Catholic Church have power based in the office, which is characteristic of stratified societies. In anthropological terminology, based on Weber's model of priests and prophets (1973), *priests* are part of a religious hierarchy in societies that have class differentiation and task specialization. Their authority derives from their social role. *Prophets* persuade by virtue of their charisma. In addition, *shamans* operate as entrepreneurs in relatively egalitarian societies and as mediators in stratified societies. Whereas the power of priests is vested in the office, shamans must prove their ability to control the spirits, usually by demonstrating the power to heal. Whereas priests are found only in hierarchical societies, shamans are found in all societies.

Priests are charged with maintaining the stability of the group by interpreting myths, conducting rituals, and caring for the material property of the religious order. Hierarchical societies typically have large religious edifices, such as temples, cathedrals, and mosques. Shamans typically operate out of their homes and deal with the everyday problems humans inevitably encounter, such as illness, bad luck, or quarrels. C. von Furer-Haimendorf contrasts the relationship of priests and shamans among the Saora of the state of Orissa in India.

The priest's special function is to maintain the cult of the local shrines and to guard the village lands from the interference of hostile spirits and sorcerers. . . . For practical purposes, however, the shaman, who may be a male or female, is the most important religious figure in a Saora village. He has the power not only to diagnose the source of trouble or disease, but to cure it. (2001, 99)

In the arts, also, rights to control the production of symbolic forms depend on whether the society is stratified or egalitarian. In stratified societies, production of art objects, music, dance, and theatrical performances is controlled by professionals. In relatively egalitarian societies, all members of the group may participate in artistic productions. This aspect of symbols and social organization will be discussed further in chapter 5.

ECONOMICS—SUBSISTENCE AND SYMBOLS

Economic systems have two major components: production and consumption. Production of goods considered necessary for human life is organized according to *patterns of subsistence*, which are systems for converting environmental resources for human use. Since they are the basis on which human life rests, subsistence patterns play a large part in shaping the way people view their physical and social universe.

Foragers are groups of people who do not produce their own food but rely on what is available in the environment; *pastoralists* depend on the animals they herd, such as sheep and cattle; *horticulturalists* cultivate gardens primarily for their own use; *agriculturalists* produce a food surplus through use of plows, irrigation, and, in many cases, fertilizer. In all these patterns of subsistence, the center of production is the home. In some cases, the food surplus generated by intensive agriculture is sufficient to support *industrialization*, which transfers the center of production from the domestic sphere to the public sphere.

The importance of subsistence in symbolic representations has been discussed by Åke Hultkrantz, who suggests that religions of North American Indians can be classified according to two overall patterns: vision quests, characteristic of hunting groups, and an emphasis on fertility, characteristic of horticultural groups, as shown in table 3.1.

Differences between the two types of religion can be correlated with lifestyles characteristic of foragers and horticulturalists. Foragers tend to be

Table 3.1. North American Indian Religions Classified by Lifestyle Pattern

Hunting Pattern	Horticultural Pattern
Animal ceremonialism	Rain and fertility ceremonies
Quest for spiritual power	Priestly ritual
Male Supreme Being	Goddesses and gods
Annual ceremony of cosmic rejuvenation	Yearly round of fertility rites
Few stationary cult places	Permanent shrines and temples
Shamanism	**Medicine society ritualism**
Life after death beyond the horizon or in the sky	Life after death in the underworld or among the clouds

Source: Hultkrantz 1987, 14; boldface in the original

relatively egalitarian and nomadic since they typically must move from place to place to follow game animals and to avoid overexploiting a particular location.

> For the lone hunter safety and success depended on the guardian spirit acquired through the vision quest. The guardian spirit was closer at hand than the high god or other spirits. The connection between a person and a protective spirit could become so intense that the person took part in the spirit's qualities and even in its life. (Hultkrantz 1987, 30)

In his discussion of Athapaskan hunters and fishermen who exploited the resources of the subarctic forests of North America, James W. Vanstone notes the importance of individualism for hunters:

> The cultures of hunting peoples must of necessity socialize individuals to a high degree of independence, since survival depends to a large degree on individual skills. From the standpoint of religion, this meant that a great deal of emphasis was placed on individual rituals rather than on community rituals. (1974, 59)

Horticulturalists, on the other hand, are more sedentary because they must stay close to their fields or gardens. This would allow them to maintain permanent shrines and, in some cases, develop a degree of stratification that would be reflected in a priesthood.

The opposition between foragers and food producers is not absolute, however. Hultkrantz notes that his is an ideal model and that "every Native American tribe has its own emphasis on one pattern or the other or in many cases a distinctive blending of the two patterns" (1987, 14–15).

FORAGERS

Because foragers rely on hunting, gathering, and fishing to provide for their needs, they tend to see the status of humans and animals—and in some cases of all of nature—as being relatively equal. Vanstone writes, "If one were to select the single most consistent feature of aboriginal northern Athapaskan magico-religious belief systems, it would be the significant reciprocal relationship that existed between men and the animals on which they were dependent for their livelihood" (1974, 59). Vanstone also speculates on the basis for the equivalency of humans and animals.

> Superior-subordinate aspects were largely absent from this relationship, possibly because of a widespread belief in reincarnation in animal form. This belief tended to blur the distinction between animals and men, and to emphasize the fact that the spirits of animals had to be placated if men were to continue their exploitative relationship to the natural environment. (1974, 59)

Bobby Lake-Thom, a Native American shaman,[2] notes that he was trained in shamanism through interaction with nature. "My different mentors made me spend a lot of time observing and interacting with nature" (1997, 26). His interaction with nature involved both subsistence activities and meditation on his experiences in the natural environment.

> I was taught to go out and study different birds in their territorial habitat. I had to remember what kind I saw, what color they were, how they behaved among themselves and with the other birds, and how they related to other creatures and their natural environment. In the meantime, different elders would tell me bird stories, about Raven, Eagle, Robin, Flickerbird, Hummingbird, Buzzard, Owl, Turkey, Grouse, Wren, and Finch. In this way I began to see some truth in the stories. I developed an understanding of the different birds and their different characters, their behavior, colors, personalities, and powers. The phenomena then became my teachers. (Lake-Thom 1997, 26)

In the process, Lake-Thom came to see birds and other animals as messengers and harbingers, in some cases guarding against dangers or providing guidance. He also acquired an animal protector. "When I need the Raven's help, I go outside and make a special prayer, hold the bird's feathers in my hand, and call out like a Raven. Usually when I do this a Raven or Crow will suddenly come in to find out what I want" (1997, 33).

The Ainu of northern Japan foraged in a rich environment with varied resources and three main ecological zones: mountains, hills, and seashore. Bears, which lived in the mountains, occupied both the highest niche in the Ainu environment and the highest place in the Ainu pantheon. Along the shore, the Ainu hunted sea mammals, including seals and sea lions. The sea was viewed as the sacred residence of the sea deities, and sea mammals were believed to be produced by a sea deity. The sea deities were not as sacred as the bear, and the sea mammals themselves were not seen as deities. Women were forbidden to participate in sea mammal hunting and sea fishing. The intermediate zone, which yielded plants and freshwater fish, was the least sacred to the Ainu, and women could fish in this zone. Gathering plants was primarily the work of women, and though the Ainu depended as much on plants as animals, plants were considered immobile and powerless and hence were not deified (Ohnuki-Tierney 1974). In the case of the Ainu, the power of the pantheon reflected the power of the plants or animals exploited by the Ainu, and that power was reflected in the sacredness of the environmental niche.

PASTORALISTS

For pastoralists, the relationship between people and animals depends to a large extent on the kind of animals they herd. In general, cattle herders tend to revere their animals, whereas sheepherders tend to view themselves as superior to animals. Even where grains are cultivated, as among African cattle herders, cattle play a greater part in the religion than plants do. Walter Goldschmidt has studied the culture of the Sebei, who once herded cattle on the north slope of an extinct volcano, Mount Elgon, in Uganda.

> The basic elements of the Sebei religion derive from its pastoralist past. This is demonstrated by the symbolic elements in their rituals: livestock, their products and their parts, the spear and the shield, many wild plants that are associated with both good and evil purposes, and *kraals* [enclosures for livestock] represented in miniature and as the location for rites. Cultivated plants play a minor role, even in the harvest *korosek* [plants thought to be health-giving or cleansing, as well as the rites in which the plants are used]. (Goldschmidt 1986, 124–25)

For the Nuer, of the southern Sudan, cattle define their social identity. The Nuer do not kill cattle for their daily diet. Instead, they derive protein from the milk and blood provided by cattle. Cattle are killed only as offerings to the gods. As is usual with animal sacrifice, cattle that have been sacrificed are eaten by the people after the gods have consumed the spiritual essence of the animals.

Middle Eastern sheepherders, on the other hand, emphasize the superiority of humans over animals and extend this relationship to the relationship of humans to God. Just as sheep are completely dependent on the shepherd, humans are completely dependent on an all-powerful God. The Basseri herd sheep along a three-hundred-mile migration route in the mountains and steppes of northern Iran. Though they are Muslim, the needs of their sheep take precedence over the ritual requirements of the Islamic calendar. Sheep must be constantly tended lest they wander off and be stolen or eaten by predators, and Basseri migration routes are hazardous. Fredrik Barth (1986) notes that Basseri pray individually rather than communally and do not hold communal religious gatherings, even on Friday, the Islamic holy day.

The Basseri are not less devout than other Muslims. However, their nomadic lifestyle, which consists of moving their sheep from highlands to lowlands on an annual cycle, does not permit the building of mosques. Furthermore, the necessity of tending the sheep around the clock prevents adherence to a rigid ritual cycle.

> The Basseri, as Shiah Moslems, accept the general premises and pro-
> scriptions of Islam to the extent that they are familiar with them. On the
> other hand, they are aware of their own laxity in these matters, and are
> generally uninterested in religion as preached by Persian mullahs, and in-
> different to metaphysical problems. (Barth 1986, 135)

Contrary to Barth's assessment, the Basseri are not "lax" in their practice of Islam. Instead, they have adapted their observance to a nomadic, ever-vigilant lifestyle. An office worker in Tehran may gain favor by stopping work to pray five times a day, but sheep are not inclined to adhere to such a schedule. The Basseri do not view their attitude toward Islam as "lax": "The Il-e-Khas, who recently rejoined the tribe after having resided in the Isfahan area 100 years, are a partial exception to this rule [of not observing Islamic ritual requirements and proscriptions], and are today criticized and somewhat despised by other Basseri as being rigidly orthodox, miserly, and humourless" (Barth 1986, 135–36).

Most Basseri rituals center on the human life cycle: birth, marriage, and death. However, informal rites are performed at shrines in the form of graves of saints, which the Basseri pass in the course of their migrations.

Few of these have any great significance to the nomads, but they usually pray or show respect as they pass by, though they often have no name, and rarely any myth about the actions of the Saint who was buried there. Nor do any of these shrines serve as centres around which larger groups congregate. Individuals may seek such shrines for prayers and special requests for help and support from the dead Saint; in the southern areas . . . are several shrines which are visited by nomads and villagers alike. (Barth 1986, 137)

The shrine of Said Mohammed, located in the summer pasture area, is an important exception to this pattern. Men, women, and children of the camp groups that regularly pass close to this shrine dress in their best clothes and visit the shrine together. Each household in the group is expected to give an animal for sacrifice. The households of a camp group then join in a meal of meat and rice, distributing a share of the feast to beggars and shrine keepers. Barth writes that "a gay and carefree feeling of a festive picnic prevails" (1986, 138).

Nomadic sheepherders such as the Basseri illustrate the importance of subsistence to the symbolic system of the group. Their nomadic lifestyle does not support the rigid ritual observances of more sedentary groups, such as horticulturalists and agriculturalists.

HORTICULTURALISTS AND AGRICULTURALISTS

Horticulturalists and agriculturalists are dependent on the land for their survival. In keeping with this dependency, the earth itself or some specific areas of the earth typically are viewed as sacred or as occupied by spirit beings. New Guinea horticulturalists maintain altars to nature spirits in their gardens. Shinto agriculturalists of Japan view certain features of the landscape as being occupied by nature spirits, or *kami*. A farmer is expected to provide food for the kami from whom he attains rights to land, much as farmers in Japan's feudal times supplied their lords with the products of their labor. Thus, the relationship between the farmer and the kami mirrors the relationship between the farmer and his lord.

The Aymara of Bolivia are horticulturalists who also herd sheep, and their symbolic system reflects the interdependency of humans, plants, and animals. Pregnant women and pregnant sheep are treated the same; care must be taken not to enrage them. Hans C. Buechler and Judith-Maria Buechler observe that "a pregnant woman is supposed to work in the fields to ensure the fertility of the fields as well as her own fertility, but a menstruating woman may not go into the fields. Menstruation, the negation of fertility in women, is related to unproductive fields" (1971, 92). The symbol of all fertility—humans, animals, and the earth—is the female deity *Pachamama*, who has attributes of human mothers. Buechler and Buechler note, "Just as human mothers are unpredictable so is *Pachamama*" (1971, 91).

The fertility of women and the earth is often linked in horticultural and agricultural societies. Malinowski describes a gardening ritual performed by Trobriand Island horticulturalists before clearing a garden in preparation for planting.

> The belly of my garden swells.
> The belly of my garden swells as with child.
> (quoted in Hays 1958, 317)

Dogon horticulturalists of Africa describe the earth as a woman lying on her back with her head to the north. She was created by the god Amma, who "took a lump of clay, squeezed it in his hand and flung it from him" (Griaule 1965, 17).

Philip L. Newman suggests that symbolic activities of Gururumba horticulturalists of New Guinea center on themes of growth and strength.

> The growing of food is much on their minds. Casual conversation frequently turns around the state of one's garden or the health of one's pigs. Many of the songs they sing concern growth. . . . Similarly, some of [their] more elaborate string figures depict plants or animals passing through phases in their growth cycle. (1965, 72)

Since physical strength is required for gardening and other activities, Newman adds, "It is a characteristic highly admired in both men and women, amounting to one of the major standards of beauty" (1965, 72).

INDUSTRIALISTS

Some agricultural societies have developed sufficient stratification and urbanization to become industrialized, and the way of life associated with industrialization is reflected in their symbolic systems. Max Weber (1958) suggested that the Protestant ethic helped nurture the rise of capitalism in post-Renaissance Europe. He noted that the Protestant values of sobriety, cleanliness, punctuality, hard work, and saving produced workers and businessmen well suited to a capitalist economy and industrialization. According to Weber, the accumulation of wealth became a mark of God's grace.

Technology has played a prominent role in symbolism in the U.S. world view, as expressed in art forms and mass media. Barry Garland, a spokesman for the Railroad Museum in Sacramento, California, and collector of railroad music, notes that railroads became a symbol of "a nation on the move" early in the twentieth century and that the sounds of train whistles and cars moving on railroad tracks shaped an entire musical genre (personal communication 1988). During the same era, artists and writers envisioned the future in technological terms.

Russell Lynes notes that the Centennial Exposition of 1876, a massive exhibit held in Philadelphia to commemorate the hundredth anniversary of the nation, included industrial products and what was then called "industrial art." The exhibit was described by its planners as a tribute to "the unparalleled advancement in science and art, and all the various appliances of human ingenuity for the refinement and comfort of man" (cited in Lynes 1980, 112). In 1932, Lewis Mumford wrote of U.S. aesthetics, "We value the positive results of science, disciplined thinking, coherent organization, collective enterprise, and that happy impersonality which is one of the highest fruits of personal development" (cited in Lynes 1980, 247–48). The Museum of Modern Art in New York held its first exhibition of "Machine Art" in 1934.

The "worship" of the machine was not restricted to the United States. In fact, machine imagery and stylistic forms are pervasive in industrialized societies. From the 1930s to the 1960s, the Hungarian-born artist Victor Vasarely produced a number of drawings and paintings in which he experimented with the relationship between form and motion. Many of his works are abstract. Even when depicting realistic forms, Vasarely imbued them with an abstract quality through the use of color and design. The art historian and critic Gaston Diehl describes a series of his paintings as "constructed like rigorous machines" (1972, 60). Diehl adds, "In an age devoured by a dominating mechanization, [Vasarely] makes an effort, logically, to answer to the current demands for speed, active driving function, precise adjustment, and rigorous construction" (1972, 90).

As the end of the second millennium approached, anxiety associated with this significant marker of time was expressed in fears of a worldwide computer crash. As will be discussed further in chapter 6, fears about a Y2K (year 2000) technology crash became symbolically associated with fears that the end of the millennium would coincide with the end of the world.

Though technology has become a dominant symbol in the art and popular culture of the United States, as well as a metaphorical theme in the art of other industrialized nations, it has not replaced other important symbols. French Impressionists such as Claude Monet and Paul Cézanne idealized rural life in their landscape paintings. Cézanne and Vincent van Gogh included factory smokestacks in their paintings of Marseille and the countryside around Arles. Gustave Caillebotte and Edouard Manet, as well as Monet and others, painted train stations and bridges. In the hands of Impressionist painters, industry appears almost bucolic.

ECONOMIC SYSTEMS—EXCHANGE

In all societies, people mark social relationships by gifts, goods, or services. The way in which we exchange material goods and services shapes our concepts of what we can expect from others and what we are expected to give in return. These exchanges are inevitably reflected in our symbolic system. In his book *The Gift*, Marcel Mauss writes that expectations about the obligations humans owe each other are expressed symbolically in their expectations of what they owe the gods and what they will receive in return. The relationship of reciprocity between humans and spirit beings, Mauss suggests, is expressed symbolically in such practices as sacrifice and the giving of alms, in which a portion of one's wealth is given to the poor.

Universally, it appears, people assume that gods or other spirit beings are entitled to some form of tribute from human beings. This may take the form of offerings of food, incense, or other material goods; money; or some form of service. Sacrifice of animals or humans is usually associated with the idea of the need to feed the gods. In some cases, offerings and sacrifice are based on a view of spirit beings as the source of human life and material goods. Offerings and sacrifice may also be considered necessary for maintaining cordial relationships with spirit beings or to appease them for wrongdoing.

Mauss considers alms an indirect payment of tribute owed to the gods: "Alms are the result on the one hand of a moral idea about gifts and wealth and on the other of an idea about sacrifice. . . . [In the giving of alms,] the gods and spirits consent that the portion reserved for them and destroyed in . . . sacrifice should go to the poor and the children" (1967, 15–16). Mauss implies that alms are equivalent to sacrifice diverted to serve social needs.

Mundugumor horticulturalists of New Guinea, studied by Margaret Mead, based their relationship to spirit beings on the principle of *balanced reciprocity*: "If one broke a taboo imposed by a water spirit, then one became ill; if one made the proper offering to that spirit, one would recover" (Mc-Dowell 2001, 339). The reciprocal relationship is balanced because Mundugumor do not consider the spirit to have the option of failing to honor the implied contract established by a gift: "If a spirit accepted a particular offering, then the spirit had no choice but to make the donor well—that's the way the world works" (McDowell 2001, 339). Nancy McDowell notes that the place of reciprocity in Mundugumor religion reflected the central role of reciprocity in their economic and political systems. "Much as Westerners assume that gravity will work when they get out of bed in the morning, the Mundugumor assumed that the world operates according to the principle of reciprocity" (2001, 339).

Similarly, religions of the Judaic tradition, which include Christianity, view the relationship between humans and G-d as a contract of balanced reciprocity, expressed in the symbolism of the Ark of the Covenant. (When discussing Judaic customs, I follow the Jewish ban against using the word *God* outside a sacred context, and I observe the Christian convention of spelling out the name when writing of Christian customs.) G-d is expected to take care of His people in return for their obedience to His laws. In one of my psychological anthropology classes, I asked Christian and Jewish students how they would react if they obeyed the rules of their religion and later learned that G-d had decided not to honor His side of the contract. They said they would feel betrayed. Their reaction indicates that the contract represented by the Ark of the Covenant is viewed as binding on G-d as well as humans.

By way of contrast, Hindu beliefs reflect *generalized reciprocity*. Humans are expected to give, but the gods are not required to reciprocate in kind. The concept of *lila*, play of the gods, symbolically states that the gods are not bound to reciprocate; the universe exists as the play and entertainment of the gods. If the gods choose to behave whimsically, humans have no recourse but to accept their will. On the other hand, humans are not punished if they choose not to make offerings.

Mahatma Gandhi said of the nineteenth-century Hindu ecstatic priest Ramakrishna Paramahamsa, "Ramakrishna's life enables us to see God face to face" (cited in Hixon 1992, vii). Ramakrishna served the Goddess Kali at the Dakshineswar Temple Garden near Calcutta, beside the Ganges River. The honorific Paramahamsa means "Great Swan." One of Ramakrishna's followers, Vivekananda, introduced Hinduism to the United States at the Chicago Parliament of Religions in 1893. His subsequent lectures throughout the United States and Europe led to the formation of the Vedanta Society, the Western branch of the Ramakrishna order. Ramakrishna describes his approach to devotion to the goddess:

> When encouraging seekers to practice certain disciplines, I always tell them to sever the head and the tail from the fish before cooking it. Cut away unnecessary ritual and solemn formality. Make spirituality directly accessible, joyous, easy to practice. I tell my friends to ignore the complex preparations and ceremonies prescribed by the Vedas and the Tantras, technical forms of worship that must be completed with perfect exactitude to be effective. I advise them to enter instead directly into the very heart of Divine Presence, with all the love and intensity of their being. I cannot enjoy performing endless rounds of *mantra* on prayer beads, or laboriously counting with my fingers, increasing the numbers day by day as some form of sacrifice or austerity. I enjoy only the continuous inward remembrance of God. (Hixon 1992, 195)

I once conducted a group of students from my Comparative Religion class on a tour of the Hindu temple in Malibu. The students were educated in the Judeo-Christian tradition of balanced reciprocity, which suggests that those who do not sacrifice to G-d or who do not obey G-d's edicts do not have a right to expect favors from G-d. We were guided by a Hindu student from the same class. One of my Christian students asked the Hindu student, "How do you worship the gods?" The Hindu student replied, "You can offer money, milk, food, or flowers. You can bow before the images of the deity. Or you can walk around the image of the deity three times."

"What happens if you don't do any of those things?" the Christian student asked.

The Hindu student thought for a while and said, "Nothing." After considering the question some more, the Hindu student added, "Hinduism is a very forgiving religion."

Though in general Hindu offerings are based in generalized reciprocity, there is an implicit contract of balanced reciprocity in the formal Hindu rituals of *puja* and *prasad* conducted by priests. Puja is an offering of food, milk, incense, flowers, and other desirable goods to the gods. The gods reciprocate with prasad. In prasad, the gods imbue offerings of food, smoke, water, fire, and flowers with their essence, and these now-sacred objects are distributed among the people by the priests.

KINSHIP SYMBOLS AND THE
ORGANIZATION OF THE FAMILY

Kinship is a pervasive metaphor in symbolic systems. Symbols modeled on kinship are especially powerful because they draw on associations formed through intimate interactions within the family. Kinship is based on consanguinity (relationship by blood) and affinity (relationship by marriage). The concept of *Pachamama* among the Aymara, discussed earlier, metaphorically expresses the relationship of humans to the earth, the source of life-giving plants, as that of the consanguineal relationship of children to their mother. The religious scholar Lex Hixon describes the prevalence of mother imagery this way:

> From the most simple, basic point of view, for several years during infancy and early childhood, both female and male children relate in essentially the same mode and with the same intensity to the mother love at the core of their daily existence. The one we call father is at first simply mother number two, with bearded or abrasive face. Every longing is for mother. All sustenance is mother. Even the infant's landscape, before and after birth, is simply mother. For nine months, her heartbeat is our rhythm, our primal music. (1994, 3)

Whereas mother imagery typically draws on her role as nurturer, imagery relating to the father usually incorporates some degree of social responsibility. Judeo-Christian symbolism draws on imagery of God the Father to illustrate the relationship between God and human beings. This image is not meant to suggest that G-d has characteristics of human males, though it is seen this way by some believers. Rather, God the Father is a metaphorical image that draws an analogy based on the father-child relationship. Characteristics attributed to G-d are similar to those expected of a father. Fathers are supposed to provide for the material well-being of their children, protect them from harm, discipline them, and love them. Similarly, G-d is portrayed as the source of material blessings, a protector, a disciplinarian, and the personification of unselfish love. Just as earthly fathers can ideally be relied on, G-d can be trusted to fulfill his part of the reciprocal contract between fathers and their children.

The following poem by the thirteenth-century Sufi poet Rumi contrasts the stern role of the father with the nurturing role of the grandmother:

> The core of masculinity does not derive from being
> male,

nor friendliness from those who console.
Your old grandmother says,
"Maybe you shouldn't go to school.
You look a little pale."
Run when you hear that.
A Father's stern slaps are better.
Your bodily soul wants comforting.
The severe father wants spiritual clarity.
He scolds, but eventually
leads you into the open.
Pray for a tough instructor
to hear and act and stay within you.
We have been busy accumulating solace.
Make us afraid of how we were. (Rumi 1987, 35)

Devotees of the Hindu goddess Kali view her as the divine Mother, as expressed in the lyrics of the eighteenth-century Hindu poet Ramprasad. In his poem "I throw the dust of pure devotion into the eyes of Death," Ramprasad personifies Death as an intruder and poses metaphorically as a child protected by an all-powerful Mother:

Watch closely, Death!
I am now standing with my entire being
grounded in Mother Reality.
I am drawing a fiery boundary
with the living name of Kali.
I challenge you to cross.
I tell you, Death,
I am no premature infant of the Wisdom Mother
whom you can threaten to overpower!
You cannot snatch me away
like candy from the hands of a child
who is reduced to terror by your empty threat.
If you address one harsh word to me, Death,
you will be confronted by my terrible Mother.
Goddess Kali is the beloved destroyer.
Her furious bliss that obliterates every limit
terrorizes even Death.
Her playful poet sings:
"Fearlessly celebrating the beauty of Ma Kali,
I throw the dust of pure devotion
into the eyes of Death

and easily elude its clumsy grasp."
(Hixon 1994, 60)

Ramprasad's description of the mother standing guard over her child evokes associations of a mother lion defending her cubs or a mother bear fending off any intruder who dares to approach her offspring. The nurturing mother is not always gentle in symbolic imagery. In many cases, as explored by Ramprasad, she defies even Death to protect the offspring to whom she has transmitted Life.

THE AFFINAL RELATIONSHIP

In Hindu symbolism, the affinal relationship between the god Krishna and the human Radha is a model of devotion to the god. Radha was so enamored of Krishna that she left her husband to be with him. Radha and Krishna are frequently depicted in Hindu art as the All-Beautiful Couple. Their names are frequently chanted together as RadhaKrishna. Just as Radha set aside the conventions to be with Krishna, devotees of the god aspire to center their lives on this manifestation of the divine. Thus, the relationship of the devotee to the god is symbolically associated with that of the lover to the beloved.

Rumi similarly draws on the imagery of the lover to celebrate the relationship of the devotee to the divine:

> Someone said, "There is no dervish, or if there is a dervish,
> that dervish is not there."
> Look at a candleflame in bright noon sunlight.
> If you put cotton next to it, the cotton will burn,
> but its light has become completely mixed with the sun.
> That candlelight you can't find is what is left of a dervish.
> If you sprinkle one ounce of vinegar over
> two hundred tons of sugar,
> no one will ever taste the vinegar.
> A deer faints in the paws of a lion. The deer becomes
> another glazed expression on the face of the lion.
> These are rough metaphors for what happens to the lover.
> There's no one more openly irreverent than a lover. He, or she,
> jumps up on the scale opposite eternity and claims to balance it.
> And no one more secretly reverent.
> A grammar lesson: "The lover died."

"Lover" is subject and agent, but that can't be!
The "lover" is defunct.
Only grammatically is the dervish lover a doer.
In reality, with he or she so overcome,
so dissolved into love,
all qualities of doing-ness
disappear.
(Rumi 1987, 30)

THE GREEK EXTENDED FAMILY

The Greek pantheon of spirit beings owes much to the Greek extended family. It is even possible to trace a genealogy, though the precise nature of the relationships varies depending on which philosopher, poet, or historian recorded the stories. Variability and contradiction are not unusual in myths and folktales since most are written down after centuries of being recounted orally. Differences in detail reflect, among other things, regional variations. Though we, at a distance of time and space, may think of ancient Greece as a single entity, it was not conceptualized that way by the Greeks. Their daily experience linked them to a particular locality, with its singular vistas, resources, social networks, and daily round of activities. As is the case with Hindu deities, Greek deities and their activities are linked to places on the Greek landscape.

Generally, Greek gods and goddesses trace descent from Chaos or Kaos. Chaos does not have human characteristics, as do the other mythological entities. Chaos is variously described as a void (Hesiod, *Theogony*) or as a mass of elemental materials (Ovid, *Metamorphoses*). Chaos gave rise to a number of beings, including Gaia (Gaea or Ge), the Earth. According to Hesiod, Gaia brought forth Uranus (Heaven or Sky) as her male counterpart. The sexual union of Gaia and Uranus produced the Cyclopses, the Titans, and the Hecatonchires (Hundred-Armed). Two of the Cyclopses represent the elemental forces of Thunder and Lightning. The Titans were the progenitors of the Sun (Helius), the Moon (Selene), and Dawn (Eos).

The Titan Cronus fathered Zeus, initiating the next era of Greek deities. Zeus's union with Leto, a daughter of the Titans Coeus and Phoebe, produced Apollo and Artemis. Apollo, associated with the sun, was a model of male beauty, intellect, and manly skills, including archery and music. Artemis, associated with the moon, was a virgin hunter, the protector of nature and freedom. Unconstrained by domesticity herself, she assisted women in childbirth. With Hera, Zeus fathered a number of children, including Ares, the god of war. In some myths, Aphrodite, the goddess of love, is the sister of Zeus; in others, she is his daughter. Similarly, in some stories, Eros, the god of love, is Aphrodite's son. According to Hesiod, however, Eros was among the original divinities arising from Chaos, a version of the myth that emphasizes the primacy of erotic love.

The lives of these divinities, as chronicled by Greek poets and philosophers, would fit seamlessly into any Latin American or North American soap opera. There are tales of deception, infidelity, incest, infanticide, and parricide, as well as interminable disputes. However, just as contemporary soap operas do not accurately reflect the way most people live, we cannot look to Greek mythology as a measure of how ancient Greeks actually lived. Rather, the myths reflect, in storied form, the human potential for love, jealousy, and conflict inherent in the organization of Greek social life, especially the organization of the Greek extended family. Zeus, the patriarch, was seen as a powerful man who meddled in the lives of his children and found it difficult to resist the charms of women other than his wife, Hera. Hera was a matriarch who passionately defended her children and punished the objects of her husband's affections, while remaining loyal to her husband.

Greek myths express the human potential for passion and conflict shaped by a particular form of family organization, rather than actual human behavior. Similarly, in writing of the bloody and violent cockfight in Bali, Clifford Geertz provides a model for understanding the interrelationship among social organization, values regarding human behavior, and the expression of counterthemes in symbolic form. Of the cockfight, which engages the passions of Balinese men, Geertz observes, "It is of these emotions, thus exampled, that society is built and individuals put together" (1971, 27). Bali is a society governed in everyday life by constraint and protocol. "Balinese go to cockfights to find out what a man, usually composed, aloof, almost obsessively self-absorbed, a kind of moral autocosm, feels like when, attacked, tormented, challenged, insulted, and driven in result to the extremes of fury, he has totally triumphed or been brought totally low" (Geertz 1971, 27).

In like fashion, the exploits of Greek divinities do not provide a model for Greek family life. Rather, they present a world of potential behavior, juxtaposed to human social life, engaged in by beings who have the power to break the rules that govern ordinary human beings. Though the genealogy of the gods is based on the model of the Greek extended family, those divine beings have attributes that humans do not have: immortality and the power to indulge their destructive impulses. And as Geertz writes of Balinese men, "In the cockfight, then, the Balinese forms and discovers his temperament and his society's temper at the same time. Or, more exactly, he forms and discovers a particular face of them" (1971, 28).

SYMBOLS AND SOCIAL CONTROL

On the social level, symbols can be used to instruct, compel, and coerce. In discussing the role of symbols in ritual, Turner observes that "ritual . . . is precisely a mechanism that periodically converts the obligatory into the desirable" (1967, 30). Individuals cannot escape the rules that society imposes on them, but symbols make the rules more palatable and provide a medium for negotiation.

George J. Klima (1970) describes a case of symbolic negotiation of conflict among the Barabaig, cattle herders of Tanzania, in Africa. The Barabaig permit an exchange of cattle, the *gefurdyed*, a form of balanced reciprocity. The exchange occurs only under certain circumstances. A man who needs a bull to use in sacrifice or to provide meat for a convalescent mother gives a pregnant cow to the owner of a suitable bull, with the understanding that the cow will be returned to the owner after the calf is born, leaving the calf as compensation for the bull.

During Klima's fieldwork, a man named Dengu needed a bull to slaughter to feed his wife, who was recovering from a difficult childbirth. He exchanged a pregnant cow for a bull from the herd of Gilagwend, a member of a rain-making clan. After the calf was born, Dengu reclaimed the cow from Gilagwend's herd, which was now being tended by a cowherd. Dengu did not tell Gilagwend that he had reclaimed the cow. Dengu later noticed that Gilagwend had become senile. In addition, the calf Dengu supplied to Gilagwend's herd had become a prolific breeder and had produced several equally prolific cows. Dengu claimed that Gilagwend had never returned the cow and claimed that he was entitled to all its progeny, taking the claim to a court of Barabaig elders. Dengu, Gilagwend, and the cowherd were required to take an oath in which each licked the blade of a spear. Parallel to the North American metaphor that justice should be blind, a spear owned by a man blinded in one eye is the preferred oracle in these cases.

While awaiting the results of the oracle, elders became concerned when the expected rains did not appear, and they accused the rainmaker Gilagwend of holding back the rains. Gilagwend protested his innocence by saying, "If it is my hand, may my home be destroyed" (Klima 1970, 31).

Within days Gilagwend's first wife died, and he died several days later. The elders considered this proof that Gilagwend had lied about holding back the rains and had also lied during the spear licking oath. Dengu claimed the twelve head of cattle produced by the calf he had transferred to Gilagwend in exchange for the bull. Gilagwend's second wife appealed to the court, winning six cattle to be distributed among Gilagwend's survivors.

As the drought continued, grass failed to grow in sufficient quantity, and the milk supply of cows declined. Gilagwend's second wife went to the government-appointed chief and asked him to administer an oath to herself and Dengu, which required them to lick the blood drawn from the cut ear of one of Dengu's six cows. Dengu was afraid to take this oath, so he offered the chief a bribe to decide the case in his favor. Dengu then refused to pay the bribe, and the drought continued. The chief appealed to the council of elders, which pronounced a death curse on Dengu. Klima writes, "He continued to live, although lonely and shunned by everyone except his nearest kin. . . . Dengu is a tragic figure of a man whose avarice led him to a life of social isolation" (1970, 32).

Dengu at first appeared to win the social negotiation by relying on deception and manipulation of social mores in an attempt to gain the advantage in a dispute over property. Eventually, however, Dengu fell prey to dangers on both the social and the symbolic/spiritual levels. He failed to keep two social contracts: his commitment to repay the loan of a bull through the gift of a calf and his offer of a bribe to the tribal chief. A series of natural disasters provided culturally appropriate evidence that Dengu's betrayal involved not only the social order but the relationship of human beings to the universe as a whole.

SYMBOLS AS SOCIAL AND CULTURAL BOUNDARIES

My Hungarian-Croatian friend Gizella lamented the fact that I had chosen to spend Christmas with my son and his family rather than with her and her family. She was so distressed, she said, that her husband jokingly suggested that we should celebrate the Serbian Christmas together on January 7. "That sounds good," I naïvely told Gizella when I returned from my more conventional (for North America) Christmas holiday. "No," she said, laughing but adamant, "they would bomb him."

The "they" Gizella referred to were fellow Croats who lived in the neighborhood. Before the dissolution of Yugoslavia, Croatian and Serbian expatriates lived amicably together as neighbors and as equal members of the Dalmatian Club, which served immigrants and their descendants from the Dalmatian Coast of Yugoslavia. The dissolution of Yugoslavia among factions of Serbs, Croats, and other groups was reflected in schisms that developed in the expatriate community in the California town of San Pedro. Had Gizella's husband observed the Serbian Christmas, his fellow Croats would have viewed him as a traitor.

According to Gizella, the factionalism that developed among expatriates from her native Yugoslavia, now Croatia, destroyed her Christmas since half her friends—the Serbian half—disappeared from her social circle. Emotions ran so high between the two formerly interacting groups that the symbolic act of observing a Serbian Christmas could conceivably lead to death—social if not literal—for an expatriate Croat. Long after political and economic barriers have fallen, ethnic groups preserve symbolic events as representative of their unique identity.

Gizella's account of the importance of the boundary between Yugoslavia/Serbia and Croatia was borne out on two other occasions. I mentioned to a Croatian acquaintance, "I'm not sure whether to refer to this [segment of the country] as Yugoslavia or Croatia, since it was part of Yugoslavia when I traveled there."

"It's Croatia," he replied.

"But it was part of Yugoslavia when I traveled there," I protested.

"It has *always been* Croatia," he responded.

On the other occasion, I was standing in the checkout line of a market that serves both Croats and Serbs at Christmas time. "What is it with the red Santa Claus suits?" a Serbian woman demanded.

"It's an American custom," I replied in an attempt at conciliation.

"It is *not* Christmas," she retorted.

Gizella and I reached a compromise with respect to celebrating the holidays together. "Why don't we celebrate New Year's Eve together?" I suggested after realizing that the concept of celebrating a Serbian Christmas was unworkable. "Yes," she agreed. "But we will celebrate it the Croatian way."

SYMBOLIC ANTAGONISM

Symbols exclude as well as include. The same symbols that promote multiple levels of communication and a sense of community within a group can send a powerful message of exclusion to outsiders. In many cases, that can lead to violence. Among Buddhists and Hindus, the swastika is an important symbol of well-being and unity. The Sanskrit word "swastika" means "he is well." The swastika is used to adorn statues and temples. Early in the twentieth century, the German dictator Adolf Hitler co-opted the swastika as a symbol of Aryan exclusivism. For Jews and others persecuted in Nazi Germany, it became a symbol that evokes the horrors of concentration camps and revives memories of family members who died in those camps.

Buddhist and Jewish associations with the swastika collided in Los Angeles early in the 1990s, after Vietnamese immigrants erected a Buddhist temple in the San Fernando Valley. The entry to the temple grounds was guarded by wrought iron gates that bore a large swastika. The emblem became a cause célèbre when Jewish neighbors objected to the symbol on the grounds that it was anti-Semitic. Negotiations with monks residing at the temple produced no agreement. The monks stated that, though they respected the views of their Jewish neighbors, the swastika was an important part of their own religion. The public debate came to an end when the gate was blown up late one night.

The swastika—and the varying emotional reactions to it—illustrates the importance of culture and context in understanding and interpreting symbols. Over the course of human history, many millions of people have died for symbols, and they will continue to do so. It is virtually impossible to hold a rational discourse where symbols are at stake because symbols draw on powerful unconscious associations. Ironically, the same symbols that promote identification within a group may evoke hostilities at its boundaries. Where symbols mark cultural boundaries between groups—as all symbols do—it is difficult to avoid rancor and strife.

NOTES

1. See Robert Reynolds, http://www.aquinas~multimedia.com/cards/cards/html.

2. I owe this reference to Steve Rosales, a student in my introductory cultural anthropology class at El Camino College.

4

SYMBOLS AND RELIGION

Religion is a universal among human groups. In general, religion is defined as a symbolic system dealing with the relationship of human beings to the supernatural, to divine or spirit beings, or to matters that transcend mundane reality. As Anthony F. C. Wallace puts it, "It is the premise of every religion—and this premise is religion's defining characteristic—that souls, supernatural beings, and supernatural forces exist" (1966, 52).

Durkheim distinguished religion from magic, which may have similar beliefs and practices, on the basis that religion is focused on the level of the group, whereas magic is individualistic. Magic, Durkheim wrote, does not generate lasting bonds between "the magician and the individuals who consult him" (1915, 60). Durkheim adds: "*There is no Church of magic*" (1915, 70, italics in the original).

In contemporary usage, religion and magic are distinguished according to purpose. The primary purpose of religion is explanation, whereas magic is aimed at manipulation. According to Malinowski, religion formulates and promotes a way of thinking that helps the individual deal with difficulties in everyday life and cope with the certainty of death.

> Religious faith establishes, fixes, and enhances all valuable mental attitudes, such as reverence for tradition, harmony with environment, courage and confidence in the struggle with difficulties and at the prospect of death. This belief, embodied and maintained by cult and ceremonial, has an immense biological value, and so reveals to primitive man truth in the wider, pragmatic sense of the word. (1954, 89–90)

Aspects of religion studied by anthropologists are myths or mythology, ritual, and the organization of the religious community. Since the social organization of religion was discussed in chapter 3, the present chapter will focus on myth and ritual. Myths are symbolic stories that reflect the world view and values of a group of people, as well as their social organization. In general, ritual is symbolic behavior associated with religion and magic. The Native American shaman Bobby Lake-Thom provides an instructive synopsis of the relationship between myth and ritual as reflected in the experience of the original peoples of North America:

> Nature was the native people's laboratory and school. The concept of "power" was a significant part of the learning process. Myth served as a form of theory while ritual provided one with the opportunity to experience, synthesize, and internalize power. Our ancestors realized that the world was a Great Mystery, and could not be easily explained. It was complicated and very powerful. In order to survive, adapt, and succeed in life, one had to have power of one's own: a supernatural power such as one of the "relations" in Nature, an ancestral ghost, a special spirit guide, or a creation of one's imaginary guilt/aid. (Lake-Thom 1997, 49)

Durkheim would have described this "Great Mystery" as the power of society to direct human lives, but he would not have quarreled with Lake-Thom's analysis of the role of myth and ritual in comprehending and coping with this "power."

MYTHOLOGY

"In the beginning God created the heaven and the earth. And the earth was without form, and void; and darkness *was* upon the face of the deep. And the Spirit of God moved upon the face of the waters" (Genesis 1:1–2). This is an account of the beginning of the universe familiar to most people in North America. To anthropologists, this is a myth, a story that conveys symbolic truths about how a particular group experiences the world.

Myths describe the nature of the universe, both natural and supernatural, and define the place of human beings within this symbolic landscape. In many cases, the symbolic landscape conforms in general outline to the physical landscape occupied by the group that has given rise to the myth. The myth describes the landscape in terms of its meaning for the people who occupy it. A myth also defines the obligations people owe to each other; to the plants, animals, and geographical features that make up the landscape; and to the spirit entity or beings that created the landscape and established the order of the universe. In the following pages we will discuss creation myths, beliefs about the nature of the universe (cosmology), and beliefs about the nature of human beings, drawing on some ethnographic examples.

CREATION MYTHS

Creation myths are symbolic stories describing how the universe and its inhabitants came to be. Creation myths develop through oral traditions and therefore typically have multiple versions. Variations in a particular creation myth reflect differences in language and regional affiliations. Though they may appear to be simply adventure stories about things that happened in the past, creation myths continue to have relevance by providing a social charter in describing how human society came to be. That is, they validate the contemporary social order by tracing it to a sacred social ordering in the past.

Harold Courlander compiled the following creation myth of the Hopis of what is now the U.S. Southwest by interviewing elders of the First, Second, and Third Mesas:

> In the beginning there was only Tokpella, Endless Space. Nothing stirred because there were no winds. No shadows fell because there was no light, and all was still. Only Tawa, the Sun Spirit, existed, along with some lesser gods. Tawa contemplated on the universe of space without objects or life, and he regretted that it was so barren. (1971, 17)

The creation myth then explains why Hopi society came to take its present form. It illustrates the role of creation myths in infusing contemporary societies with meaning and authenticity.

The First World

Tawa created the First World by gathering the elements of Endless Space and infusing them with some of his own substance. There were no people in the First World, only insect-like creatures who lived in a dark cave deep in the earth (Courlander 1971, 17).

Tawa was deeply disappointed in his creation because the creatures did not understand the meaning of life. He sent Gogyeng Sowuhti, Spider Grandmother, to earth to lead the creatures into another great cave far above the first one. As they journeyed, Tawa changed the creatures into be-ings that somewhat resembled dogs, coyotes, and bears. "There was fur on their bodies, their fingers were webbed, and they had tails" (Courlander 1971, 18). The creatures were happy in the Second World for a while but soon began quarreling. Tawa once again sent Spider Grandmother to lead the creatures on a journey. This part of the creation myth conveys the idea that conflict displeases the Creator.

The First People

While the creatures traveled, Tawa created the Third World, which had a lighter atmosphere than the Second World and also had water, which the creatures would use to water their fields. This part of the myth establishes horticulture as the Hopi way of life. As the creatures journeyed with Spider Grandmother, their fur, webbed fingers, and tails disappeared. Spider Grand-mother said to them, "Now you are no longer merely creatures. You are people. Tawa has given you this place so that you may live in harmony and forget all evil. Do not injure one another. Remember that Tawa created you out of Endless Space, and try to understand the meaning of things" (Cour-lander 1971, 18). At this point, the people were provided with a blueprint for living their lives.

The people made villages, planted corn, and lived in harmony in the Third World, grateful to the Sun Spirit who had created them and given them a new world. "Yet things were not perfect. There was a chill in the air, and the light was only a grayness" (Courlander 1971, 18). Spider Grand-mother taught people how to weave blankets and cloth to stay warm, and she taught the women to make pots out of clay so they could store water and food. "But the pots could not be baked and they broke easily. And the corn did not grow very well because warmth was lacking" (Courlander 1971, 18).

A hummingbird sent by Masauwu, Ruler of the Upper World, Care-taker of the Place of the Dead, and Owner of Fire, showed the people how to create fire. The people made fires around their fields, and the warmth made their corn grow. Once, when they became careless, a fire burned a nearby house. When the ashes were cool, the people found their pots did not break so easily. Thus, the people learned how to fire pottery to make it hard and how to cook their meat instead of eating it raw. Life was much better for people in the Third World until the *powakas* (sorcerers) began to sow discontent and turn the people's minds away from virtuous things.

Tales of the first three worlds of the Hopis explain what is valuable in human life by providing a negative lesson. The first creatures were unsatisfactory because they did not understand the meaning of life. Creatures of the Second World were unsatisfactory both because they did not understand the meaning of life and because they quarreled among themselves. The story of the Third World builds on this model and illustrates the type of behavior and attitudes valued by the Hopis. As the creatures became people, their lives centered on horticulture, and they acquired skills important to their way of life: weaving blankets and cloth, making and firing pottery, tending their fields, and cooking meat. But a new source of problems arose: sorcerers, who began to deliberately sow disharmony.

The First Sorcerers

The orderly and peaceful conduct of life in the Third World was disrupted by the actions of sorcerers. The tale of the dissolution of the Third World teaches about social life by explicitly stating what went wrong:

> The younger people grew disrespectful of the older. Husbands sought other women, and wives sought other men. Instead of caring for their fields, men spent their time in the kivas [ceremonial structures] gambling. And instead of grinding corn, women went into the kivas to join the men. Children wandered around unclean and uncared for, and babies cried for milk. What a man wanted he would take from another instead of fashioning it for himself. . . . Instead of seeking to understand the meaning of life, many began to believe that they had created themselves. (Courlander 1971, 19)

Through an economy of images, this part of the Hopi creation myth provides a model of human social life that defines behavior expected of men and women as workers and as husbands and wives. It also establishes the relationship of younger people to elders, of parents to children, of neighbor to neighbor, and of humans to their creator.

In upsetting the virtuous order of things, the sorcerers demonstrated the destructive nature of evil: "The cornstalks in the fields withered before the ears were formed. The flowing rivers moved more sluggishly and the springs dried up. Clouds drifted over the fields but did not release their rain. Squash and melon vines stopped growing, and sickness came into many houses" (Courlander 1971, 20). In an environment where water is scarce and precious, evil is represented symbolically by lack of water.

A few elders who remembered that Tawa was their father met in *kivas* to discuss the sad nature of things and tried to change things, but nothing changed. "There was evil and chaos all around them" (Courlander 1971, 20). Once again, Tawa sent Spider Grandmother to earth. This time, she did not lead the people to a new place. Instead, she helped them to find a new place for themselves. She said to them, "Tawa, the Sun Spirit, is displeased with what he has created. The powakas have made you forget what you should have remembered. Therefore, all people of good heart should go away from this place and leave the evil ones behind" (Courlander 1971, 20). At this stage, in becoming fully human, the Hopis had to take responsibility for their own well-being.

The Importance of Elders, Medicine Men, and Brides

The people consulted among themselves and were troubled. Some asked, "Where can we go? Is there another place?" Then an old man said, "Have we not heard footsteps in the sky, as though someone is walking there?" Other old men confirmed that they had heard footsteps in the sky. The people agreed to send a messenger to discover whether they could survive in the place above them. They called the medicine men, who filled a pipe and smoked it, passing it from one to another until their minds were tranquil.

The medicine men gathered some clay and shaped it into the form of a bird. They placed the bird on a *kwatskiavu* cloth, a robe made for brides, and covered the bird with an *ova* cloth, a bride's shawl used in rituals. The medicine men sat in a circle holding the edges of the shawl, singing, and moving it gently up and down. They placed their hands under the cloth and worked secret magic. When they removed the *ova* cloth, a living swallow sat where the clay bird had been before.

The swallow was sent to explore the world that lay above the sky. The bird flew high enough to see an opening in the sky but could go no farther. He returned to the people and fluttered weakly to the ground, saying, "I found an opening in the sky. It was as though I were looking up through the entrance of a kiva. But my strength failed and so I had to return" (Courlander 1971, 21).

This part of the story validates the social roles of the male elders and medicine men, as well as the importance of the kiva. It is in the kiva, the ceremonial site for consultation among males, that male elders point the way to the new world, and the messenger is created through the magical powers of the medicine men. This part of the creation myth also establishes the role of animals as helpers, thus prefiguring the importance of animals in Hopi travels in the Fourth World and the rise of Hopi clans.

It also symbolically establishes the importance of brides as a source of future life. Just as infants develop under the fertile mantle of brides and eventually emerge as living beings, the swallow emerges fully alive from under the ritual clothing of brides. This part of the myth also establishes the complementary role of men and women in creation. Men place the knowledge-bearing but inert material, which is potential life, under the bride's mantle, where it remains until it acquires life, assisted by the ritual activities of males. In other Hopi stories, the life-harboring womb is equated with the earth, which is impregnated by a knowledge-bearing digging stick skillfully wielded by males. The seed remains hidden in the ground until it emerges as a new living being.

The next part of the story continues to describe the cooperative effort necessary to bring forth life. The medicine men made a white dove, which was strong enough to pass through the opening in the sky but could not see living creatures in the Fourth World. The medicine men then created a hawk and finally a catbird. The catbird flew to a place of sand and mesas: "He saw large fires burning alongside gardens of squash, melons and corn. Beyond that was a single house made of stone. A person was sitting there, his head down, sleeping" (Courlander 1971, 21). The catbird alit by the sleeping man, who awoke and raised his head, revealing his face:

> His eyes were sunken in deeply, there was no hair on his head, and his face was seared by burns and encrusted with dried blood. Across the bridge of his nose and his cheekbones two black lines were painted. Around his neck were two heavy necklaces, one made of four strands of turquoise, the other of bones. (Courlander 1971, 21)

The catbird recognized the man as Masauwu, Spirit of Death, Owner of Fire, and Master of the Upper World.

The Emergence of Tribes

The people were assisted in their journey to the Fourth World by Spider Grandmother and her two grandsons, the warrior gods Pokanghoya and Polongahoya, aided by a chipmunk and a mockingbird. As the people emerged into the Fourth World, Yawpa the mockingbird stood at Spider Grandmother's side and assigned to each of them a tribe and a language, giving each a direction to go in migration. To one, the mockingbird said, "You shall be a Hopi and speak the Hopi language." To another, he said,

"You shall be a Navajo and speak the Navajo language," and so on, until he had also named the Paiutes, the Zunis, the Supais, the Pimas, the Utes, the Comanches, the Sioux, and the White People (Courlander 1971, 24).

Spider Grandmother and her two grandsons then created important features of the landscape and showed the elders and medicine men how to establish the sun and moon in the sky, bringing light to the Fourth World. After four days, the people were ready to move on to their various places on earth, but the village chief's son died, which led to the discovery that a sorceress was among them. She was the last person who had come through the hole from the Third World. The village chief was about to throw her back into the Lower World, but she pleaded with the people to let her stay. She told the chief his son was not truly dead even though his body was buried under stones in the Upper World. She urged the chief to look through the hole to the Third World. When he did so, he saw that his son lived on in the Lower World.

The people argued among themselves about whether they should throw the sorceress back into the Third World. Then one of the old men suggested that they let her stay. "Good and evil are everywhere," he said. "From the beginning to the end of time good and evil must struggle against each other. So let the woman stay. But she may not go with us. After we have gone she may go wherever she wishes" (Courlander 1971, 29).

The Hopi Way of Life

As the people prepared to go their separate ways, the mockingbird asked them to choose the corn that would shape their way of life. One ear of corn was yellow, one was white, one was red, one was gray, some were speckled, one was a stubby ear with blue kernels, and one was not quite corn but merely grass with seeds at the top.

The mockingbird said, "The one who chooses the yellow ear will have a life full of enjoyment and prosperity, but his span of life will be small. The short ear with the blue kernels will bring a life full of work and hardship, but the years will be many" (Courlander 1971, 29–30). The Navajo leader quickly took the yellow ear that would bring a short life full of enjoyment and prosperity. When all the others had chosen, the leader of the Hopis picked up the short blue ear of corn, saying: "We were slow in choosing. Therefore we must take the smallest ear of all. We shall have a life of hardship, but it will be a long-lasting life. Other tribes may perish, but we, the Hopis, will survive all adversities" (Courlander 1971, 30).

When all the others had gone on the way indicated by the corn they had chosen, only the Hopis and Bahanas (White People) remained, along with the sorceress. The Hopis refused to let the sorceress go with them, but the leader of the Bahanas said, "Let the powaka come with us. Even though she is evil she has great knowledge. We do not fear her. Her knowledge will be useful to the people" (Courlander 1971, 30). Then the Bahanas left and went toward the south, followed by the sorceress. The Hopi leader said:

> Because the powaka has gone with the Bahanas, they will grow strong. They will learn evil as well as good, and they will have secrets that are not known to us. Therefore, whenever we meet with the Bahanas let us listen with caution to what they say. Let us stand apart from their ways. However, it is said that in some distant time a certain Bahana whose name is not yet known will arrive among us from the direction of the rising sun, bringing friendship, harmony and good fortune to our people. When the time comes, he will appear. Let us watch for him. Let the dead be buried with their faces toward the east so that they will meet him when he approaches. (Courlander 1971, 31)

Accounts of the early days in the Fourth World reflect an accommodation to the harsh conditions of contemporary Hopi life. The episode recounting the death of the village chief's son assures the people that death is not the end of life. Events relating to the sorceress explain why evil continues to plague people and that people must continue to struggle against conflict and reflect upon the true meaning of life. The story of drawing the small blue ear of corn explains the struggle of horticulturalists amid harsh conditions in an arid region. Finally, the association of the sorceress with the Bahanas explains the harsh treatment of Hopis by white people and offers a chance of reconciliation.

COSMOLOGY

To Dogon horticulturalists of central Africa, the world is organized in the form of a granary like those the Dogon use to store their harvested grain. The universe—and the Dogon granary—is in the form of an upside-down basket, with a round base and a square top. (When a Dogon basket is upright, the closed square bottom forms the base, and the round open end is at the top.) The circular base of the world granary represents the sun; the square roof represents the sky. The granary also represents the human body and the generative power of women.

In the celestial granary, four stairways of ten steps each rise from the round base to the square top, and each stairway faces a cardinal direction. At the sixth step of the north-facing stairway, a doorway opens to the interior, where eight chambers are arranged on two floors (Griaule 1965, 32). Each of the interior compartments of the celestial granary contains one of the eight seeds given by God to the ancestors of the Dogon clans in the order the seeds were given (Griaule 1965, 38). The eight compartments also represent the eight principal organs of the Spirit of Water, which correspond to human organs, except that the Spirit of Water also has a gizzard because it travels with the speed of birds. A round jar in the center of the bottom level symbolizes the womb. On top of this jar is a smaller jar containing the oil of a fruit associated with females. The smaller jar represents the fetus. On top of the smaller jar is a still-smaller jar containing perfume, and on top of the last is a double cup.

> All the eight organs were held in place by the outer walls and the inner partitions which symbolized the skeleton. The four uprights ending in the corners of the square roof were the arms and legs. Thus the granary was like a woman, lying on her back (representing the sun) with her arms and legs raised and supporting the roof (representing the sky). The two legs were on the north side, and the door at the sixth step marked the sexual parts. (Griaule 1965, 39)

The exterior parts of the granary symbolize the beings of the world and the place of humans in the universe. The treads of each step of the stairways are female and the risers are male; thus, they represent the offspring of the eight ancestors. The stairways themselves hold types of living beings and are associated with constellations or celestial bodies. The north stairway holds humans and fishes and is associated with the Pleiades. The south stairway is for domestic animals and is associated with Orion's belt. The east stairway is for birds and is associated with Venus, and the west stairway is for wild animals, vegetables, and insects and is associated with the "Long-tailed star" (perhaps a comet).

Both the Hopis and the Dogons are horticulturalists, and their mythology reflects the centrality of planting and, in the case of the Dogon, storing grain. A key point in the creation myth of the Hopis occurs during the Third World, when water is made available to water their fields. This is also when the creatures become people. The Hopi way of life was determined when they chose the small blue corn. For the Dogon, the form of the universe and the architecture of the granary represent the fertility of women.

The Nature of Human Beings

In Dogon mythology, the ideal birth is twins—one female, the other male—thus uniting the creative potential of the universe. Since this ideal of perfection is not always achieved, each human is born with two souls, one female, the other male. The Nummo—female and male spirits born from the union of Amma (God) with the female earth—trace on the ground beside a woman in childbirth the dual souls of an infant about to be born. The souls are implanted in a newborn child by holding it by the thighs above the place of the drawings with its hands and feet touching the ground. The female soul of a male is located in the prepuce or foreskin; the male soul of a female is located in the clitoris.

A child is socialized into its appropriate gender role by its family but remains spiritually androgynous until its opposite gender soul is surgically removed in puberty rites, when boys are circumcised and the clitoris of girls is excised. Prior to circumcision, children are viewed as unruly because the influence of the two souls makes them unstable. One of Marcel Griaule's key informants, Koguem, observes, "The uncircumcised think of nothing but disorder and nuisance" (1965, 155).

"MAKING" MEN

Koguem's view of the uncircumcised (uninitiated) as inherently disorderly is similar to the Creek worldview as described by Amelia Rector Bell. In Creek mythology, Corn Mother "feeds her children from corn that grows on her legs and is scraped off daily" (Bell 1993, 28). When Corn Mother's male children are old enough to learn that the corn they consume is scraped from her legs, they are horrified and kill her. They flee and live as warriors in the forest. Thus, the story sets up an opposition between the Corn Mother of agriculture, associated with female fertility, and life in the forest, where men live by killing animals.

Bell notes, "The unmarked category of Creek life is female. Men are 'made' through ritual processes that separate them physically and existentially from their mothers" (1993, 31). Babies of both sexes are considered female and conceptualized as lacking the phallus. Creek are matrilineal, and children are given names from their mother's clan. At the green corn ceremony, pubescent boys (but not girls) are given war names from their father's clan. The Corn Mother myth and naming customs reflect the importance of the matrilineage as the generative source while establishing for males an identity distinct from the female realm.

Creek women are seen as "food makers," a state that is characterized by *sófki:*, a watery corn gruel. Bell notes, "The strong smell of *sófki:* contrasts with the strong smell of menstruation" (1993, 31). Both smells indicate the presence of a woman, but the smell of sófki: marks the presence of a good, controlled woman whereas the smell of menstruation marks the presence of a dangerous, uncontrolled woman.

> For Creeks, female generativity and unboundedness, made explicit in menstruation, provide the basic growth principle that is life's force and vitality. Men's ability to define and shape social form is demonstrated through identification with fire, sun's light, logs, bones and instruments for combat. The politics of gendered subjectivity ramify throughout Creek social action and speech. (Bell 1993, 35)

For Creeks, language is associated with definition of social realms. A child acquires "bones" and separates from undifferentiated femininity when it begins to speak. From that point, the child is expected to walk by itself and will no longer be carried. Public oration is the exclusive province of men.

The opposition between female generativity and male social differentiation is acted out symbolically in stomp dances held at ceremonial grounds from March to November. Both men and women dance, but only men sing. Women shake turtleshell rattles strapped to their legs. "Participants in the dance seek to become 'one body'—a harmonious and well-choreographed group uniting men and women, hosts and allies" (Bell 1993, 29). Thus, the Creek view of a male social order crafted from female generativity is symbolically expressed in the imagery of the Corn Mother myth and acted out ritually in the stomp dance.

RITUAL

Before batting, many professional baseball players tap the plate in a precise sequence. They believe this symbolic act aids their performance at bat. Before every race, the auto racer Jackie Stewart ritually removed his watch and entrusted it to the captain of his racing team, a symbolic promise to return.

Athletes in the injury-prone sports of ice hockey and American football use rituals to protect themselves against injury and poor performance.

Anthropologists have long noted that ritual is associated with high-risk situations, including those that involve physical danger, danger of failure, and social complexity. The performance of ritual influences the performance of hazardous tasks, the formation of human groups, and the ability of humans to undergo life crises. Though there has been much debate about the nature and purpose of ritual, most anthropologists would agree that ritual is

1. Repetitive—Ritual occurs again and again in a given context, and/ or certain elements tend to be repeated throughout the behavioral sequence.
2. Stylized—Ritual is formal rather than spontaneous.
3. Sequential—There is an orderly progression from beginning to end. Transposition of elements within a ritual is believed to diminish its efficacy. In some cases, varying the order of a ritual may be seen as disrespectful or dangerous.
4. Nonordinary—Ritual is distinct from mundane activities and/or is not essential to technical performance. Rituals typically are enacted at a time and place set apart as sacred or powerful. In addition, Sally F. Moore and Barbara Myerhoff write, "Actions . . . used are extraordinary themselves, or ordinary ones are used in an unusual way, a way that calls attention to them and sets them apart from other, mundane uses" (1977, 7). For example, the communion wafer used in the Roman Catholic Mass is ritually consecrated; it is not the same as a piece of toast served at breakfast, though both the wafer and the toast are bread.
5. Potent—Ritual is believed to be either innately powerful or powerful in controlling supernatural beings or forces.

Athletes practice or warm up before a game because these activities "work" on a technical level by helping them to maintain their physical fitness. They perform their "routine" or ritual because "it works" on a symbolic level by helping them to achieve the psychological state necessary for competition. The ritual "works" because it is associated with past success, but this is not the only criterion for performing a particular ritual. The success of the ritual in producing measurable results in athletic competition is the external validation for the athlete's internal conviction that his rituals help him focus on the game and perform at the peak of his ability. Or as athletes sometimes phrase it, the "routine" helps them "give 110 percent." Rituals also allow an athlete to assert his identity and reinforce his social position in a complex group that includes teammates, team officials, sports writers, fans, and nearly always last in an athlete's life, members of his own family (see Womack 1982, 1992).

Though all rituals "work" in the sense that they address psychological and social processes, not all rituals "work" in precisely the same way. Here we will discuss five types of ritual that address specific contexts: rites of passage, rites of intensification, divination rites, rites of preparation, and rites of protection.

RITES OF PASSAGE

Arnold van Gennep (1960) provided the model scholars now use to analyze rites of passage, which conduct individuals and groups through times of crisis. Rites of passage are what Victor Turner calls life-crisis rituals, "designed to mark the transition from one phase of life to another" (1967, 7). Rites of passage include baptisms, naming ceremonies, puberty rites, weddings, ordination to religious office, and funerals. In North America, some subcultural rites of passage include the Bar Mitzvah, a male puberty rite among Jews, and First Communion, for Roman Catholic children. Mexican Americans and others stage elaborate *quinceaneras* marking the fifteenth birthday of their daughters.

Van Gennep identified three phases of rites of passage: separation from the old social status; a period of liminality or marginality, in which the individual has no clearly defined social identity; and aggregation or integration into the new social status. Turner (1967) built on Van Gennep's model of rites of passage in his analysis of male puberty rites among the Ndembu of northwestern Zambia. During the middle phase, Turner writes, the individual is in a liminal state, "betwixt and between," separated from his previous identity and not yet incorporated into the new identity. Typically, an individual undergoing a rite of passage is stripped of his name, an indicator of social identity, and does not acquire a new name until the aggregation phase of the rite of passage, when he acquires a new social identity.

Drawing on Mary Douglas's idea, discussed in chapter 1, that ambiguity is perceived as dangerous, Turner developed a model of the liminal state as a time of danger for both the individual and the group. During the liminal phase, the individual has no social identity and may be treated as socially dead. In some societies, initiates undergoing puberty rituals are symbolically buried. "These 'crisis' ceremonies not only concern the individual on whom they are centered, but also mark changes in the relationships of all the people connected with them" (Turner 1967, 7).

In North American wedding customs, a bride must not be seen by anyone other than her immediate family and friends before the wedding, and it is considered "bad luck" for outsiders to see either her or her dress before she walks down the aisle at the time of the wedding. The bride's liminal status is also indicated by the fact that she is veiled and walks down the middle aisle, which separates members of the bride's and groom's families. The bride is the marginal person who will unite the two kin groups by giving birth to children. The bride is unveiled by the groom after she is publicly announced as his wife. She may also take the family name of her new husband. The importance of the unveiling ceremony is indicated by the fact that the term has found its way into language usage: a new statue, building, or project may be "unveiled."

In ice hockey, a rite of passage marks a change in team affiliation: It is the custom to shave new members of a team from head to foot (see Womack 1982). Shaving of the head commonly occurs in initiation rites for priests, nuns, monks, and soldiers. Raymond Firth has described several layers of meaning of this ritual.

> Deliberate shaving of the head, or close cutting of the hair, has taken on a ritual quality, intended to mark a transition from one social state to another, and in particular to imply a modification in the status or social condition of the person whose hair is so treated. . . . In most general terms shaving the head is a sign of *tristitia* [sadness] . . . of diminution of the self. (1973, 288–90)

Firth's observation is consistent with the way hockey players talk about their custom of ritual shaving. Hockey players use the shaving ritual to enforce conformity to the group. If a new player has not been shaved, other players may taunt him by threatening him with shaving whenever he behaves in a way that inconveniences other members of the team. One young hockey player who arrived late for the bus taking the Los Angeles Kings to the airport was serenaded with the "Burma Shave" song by other members of the team. For hockey players, the shaving ritual reminds the athlete of his responsibilities to his new team.

As is true of initiation rituals cross-culturally, the way in which a hockey player reacts to the ritual shaving can affect his later standing on the team. The athlete is expected to fight off his teammates, thus increasing the danger of being cut in the process. His later status is determined by how many of his teammates it took to hold him down for the shaving. Among African cattle herders, as among other groups, the adult status of both males and females is established by the degree of stoicism with which they undergo circumcision during their puberty rituals.

Rituals of Mourning

Though North Americans generally recognize the importance of such rites of passage as weddings—and celebrate them with much fanfare—they typically underestimate the importance of rites of passage associated with death. Most societies observe an annual cycle of mourning, marked by rituals that signal each stage of the mourning process. On the death of a chief, people of the Trobriand Islands of New Guinea observe taboos against shouting and wearing flowers or vividly colored clothing. Women shave their heads, paint their bodies with blackened powder from burnt coconut husks, cry, and "chant the traditional mourning sounds that convey their sadness and longing" (Weiner 1988, 19). From the moment anyone's death appears imminent, normal life comes to a halt.

> There is no village sound more chilling than the shrill, poignant cries announcing a death. Even when a person is seriously ill and everyone knows that death is imminent, the lamenting wails still come as a shock. The house where the dead person lies fills quickly with close relatives who throw themselves across the body, sobbing, "my mother," "my sister," or "my father," "my brother." (Weiner 1988, 30)

The extravagant display of grief by the Trobriand Islanders contrasts sharply with the restraint in the display of grief expected of many people in the United States. Jacqueline Kennedy was praised in mass media and won nationwide respect when she displayed no emotion while watching the funeral ceremonies for her assassinated husband, President John F. Kennedy. Still, the funeral ceremonies for President Kennedy and Trobriander funerary practices have some aspects in common. The entire nation paused in its activities to attend the funeral of President Kennedy in person or through some aspect of the mass media, a mark of the respect due to the country's leader. As is the case in virtually all societies, the degree of mourning display is related to the dead person's status in the community.

Annette Weiner writes of the Trobriand Islanders that "death halts all joyful activities as sharply as if a solar eclipse suddenly turned bright day into darkest night. Attention to death is swift and then drawn out over a long period of time; the deceased is far too valuable to disappear quickly from the minds and hearts of those who mourn" (1988, 33).

The body of the dying or dead person is decorated and made beautiful, Weiner says, "as if in preparation to meet a lover" (1988, 33). Before the burial, women remove a few of the dead person's fingernails and cut some of the hair, incorporating it into shell necklaces that will be worn by designated female relatives for several years "as a sign of continual mourning" (Weiner 1988, 41).

The Trobriander example contrasts with the short shrift given to the dead and the lack of support for mourners practiced by many urban North Americans. It is the custom to send flowers and cards to the bereaved, but only family members and close friends are expected to attend the funeral. In fact, more distant acquaintances are rarely made to feel welcome at a funeral. In many cases, the bereaved are discouraged from displaying grief or speaking of the death after the formal ceremonies are over. They are advised to put away their pictures of the dead person and "get on with their life."

I was criticized for continuing to display pictures of a close friend long after his memorial services were over. "When are you going to take down his pictures?" I was asked by a number of people. "When the White House takes down the picture of George Washington," I replied.

The speedy dispatch of the dead is not universal in North American society. Jews sit shivah for seven days after the funeral of a family member. The one-year anniversary of the death, the *yahrzeit*, is marked by a service at a synagogue and by burning a *yahrzeit* candle at home. Approximately one year after the death, an "unveiling" of the tombstone is marked by a simple ceremony at the gravesite, attended by family members and close friends. Many Asian Americans pay homage to their ancestors each year by symbolically feeding them. Mexican American families in Los Angeles mark special occasions by adorning the graves of deceased family members with appropriate seasonal decorations. Some hold birthday parties at the gravesite.

Far from being morbid, these celebrations recognize the continuing importance of those who have played a significant role in our lives. The importance of remembering and mourning dead relatives and friends is recognized nationally in the legal holiday of Memorial Day. For many people, however, this observance has come to be seen more as a day away from work than as an important occasion for reflecting on the meaning of our lives and the people in our lives.

Paul C. Rosenblatt, Patricia Walsh, and Douglas A. Jackson note that customs concerning the resumption of "normal, outside-the-home" activities are inconsistent in North American mourning, giving rise to confusion for both mourners and their friends or acquaintances.

> In some cases, bereaved persons delay returning to work, school, or other outside activities quite a long time after a death and are criticized for doing this. In other cases, bereaved persons return quickly to such activities and are criticized for doing this or are encouraged to blame the activities for any bereavement difficulties experienced. (1976, 108)

Cross-culturally, funeral rituals provide a symbolic means of acting out on several levels issues and anxieties related to the loss of a loved one to death. Symbolic stories about the nature of life and death can help to resolve questions about the fate of the dead person so that mourners can make sense of their loss and have a relatively safe space to speculate about their own eventual deaths. At the same time, symbolic behaviors associated with death rituals allow mourners to act out their grief, fears, and sense of loss through culturally appropriate behavior. Rosenblatt, Walsh, and Jackson suggest that "[Americans] might benefit from increased ritualization of death ceremonies in general, from practices that take into account realistically the disorganization, anger, fear, dependency, and other needs and emotions common to bereaved persons" (1976, 109).

Restoring the Balance

Funerary rites do more than address the grieving process of individuals. Through transfers of property and goods and the changes of status associated with them, mortuary rites reaffirm the solidarity and restore the balance of social groups that have suffered loss. Daryll Forde (1962) notes that "complex and protracted mortuary ceremonies" follow the deaths of senior men among Yakö horticulturalists of eastern Nigeria. Villages are organized around patriclans (patrilineal clans tracing descent from a common ancestor), and males inherit rights to farm plots and clusters of oil palms and other valuable trees through membership in these patriclans. However, movable wealth, such as money, yam harvests, livestock, and cloth, is inherited matrilineally. Males also receive most of the bridewealth payments for their sister's daughters, the women of the matrilineage. In addition, males inherit through patrilineal succession the rights to join men's associations that carry a great deal of prestige and influence.

When a senior male dies, these overlapping and competing networks of inheritance, involving both patrikin and matrikin, must all be sorted out through an elaborate system of feasting, exchange, ceremonial display, and paying of fees to various men's organizations. Forde writes of the negotiations following the death of one senior male, "It was nearly forty days after his death before the payments and feasts to the associations had been completed. Only then could the ceremony of re-making Oka's grave take place and his goods be distributed" (1962, 117–18).

When an individual undergoes a change of social status, the interrelationships of all members of the group change with it. The birth of an infant creates mothers, fathers, grandparents, siblings, aunts, and uncles, as well as many other new kin relationships. A wedding adds a whole new set of relatives to a kin group. A death leaves a social role vacant. Rites of passage restore the balance that the change of status has disrupted. Personnel may shift places, but the social order is restored. The danger of liminality, of unclear social relationships, has been abated.

RITES OF INTENSIFICATION

Rites of intensification reinforce the solidarity of the group through regular symbolic observances, usually taking place according to a daily or calendrical cycle. In many religious groups, vespers take place each evening, and some people begin each meal with a blessing or offering of thanks. Muslims pray five times a day: at daybreak, noon, mid-afternoon, sunset, and evening.

Christians and Jews observe the Sabbath with rites of intensification on a weekly basis. For most Christians, this takes place on Sunday, though a few Christian groups observe Sabbath on Saturday and Jews observe Sabbath from sundown Friday to sundown Saturday. Buddhists do not customarily conduct weekly rites of intensification, though some Buddhist groups in North America have adapted to the weekly ritual cycle because it is more suited to the work calendar of this industrialized region. More traditionally, Buddhists observe three important holidays on an annual cycle: the anniversary of the Buddha's entry into nirvana, usually in February; the Buddha's birthday, in late spring; and the day on which the Buddha began his meditation under the Bodhi Tree, which led to the framing of the basis of Buddhist belief. Hindu rites of intensification also take place on an annual basis, typically coinciding with an event in the life of a particular deity or epic hero. Since worship of particular manifestations of the deities varies widely from one part of India to another, dates for rites of intensification also vary from one region to another.

The ancient Aztecs of central Mexico maintained a ritual cycle organized around an unusually accurate calendar based on calculating both solar and day cycles. "Grand ceremonial extravaganzas" marked each of the 18 months of their solar year (Berdan 1982, 133), and other rituals were linked to their 260-day ritual calendar, which was based on combining 20 day names with the numbers 1 through 13. Combining the 365-day solar calendar with the 260-day ritual calendar produced 18,980 uniquely named days, culminating in a "new fire" ceremony marking the end of a 52-year period, or "calendar round." Frances F. Berdan tells us that "on the designated day, all fires were extinguished, and all household idols thrown out. The cooking implements and the three traditional hearthstones of each household were also discarded. The house and surrounding areas were meticulously swept and cleaned of all debris" (Berdan 1982, 119).

These meticulous cleansing rituals were followed by rigorous taboos. The taboos were especially binding on people believed vulnerable, such as pregnant women and children.

> As night fell, everyone climbed to housetops and walls, pregnant women taking care to cover their faces with maguey-leaf masks. Children were similarly masked and not allowed to doze, for if they did, and the critical cosmic rite about to be performed failed, it was believed they would be transformed into mice. (Berdan 1982, 119)

In the darkness, priests personifying the most important deities in the Aztec pantheon climbed to the summit of Uixachtlan, a mountain on the outskirts of Mexico City, now called Cerro del la Estrella ("Hill of the Star").

> At precisely midnight, one of the priests slew a captive in the traditional fashion [by cutting out the heart of the person to be sacrificed with an obsidian knife]. With a fire drill, [the priest] then proceeded to kindle a new flame in the open chest cavity of the sacrificed captive. If the fire were successfully drawn, all would be well with the universe for another 52 years. . . . If the fire did not light, the ceremony failed. This signaled the impending end of the present sun. . . . Darkness would then overcome the earth, and the *tzitzimime*, celestial monsters, would descend to earth and devour all human beings. (Berdan 1982, 119)

As this ritual took place on the mountain, all men, women, and children in the city of Tenochtitlan punctured their earlobes with sharp thorns to draw blood in penance. They then waited in darkness for the swift runners who would bring the new flame to every temple, school, and household, signaling the successful beginning of the next 52-year cycle.

DIVINATION RITES

Divination is a process of gaining information about the course of events by calling on secret information available only to spirits and supernatural beings. According to anthropologist Anthony F. C. Wallace, "Probably no human society, even in modern, thoroughly secularized urban areas, is without people who practice divination" (1966, 108). Astrology, tarot cards, and psychic readings are all forms of divination found in North America.

The Chandalar Kutchin, Athapaskan hunters on the border of Alaska and Canada, practiced a form of divination aimed at determining whether a hunt would be successful. The diviner, often an old woman, burned an arrow to charcoal and then pulverized it in her hand. The ashes were then placed either on a stone scraper or on the shoulder blade of a moose and set on fire. The diviner then covered herself and the burning charcoal with a blanket. If she could smell burning meat, the hunt would be successful. The pattern of the fire indicated the direction to be taken by the hunters (Vanstone 1974, 64–65).

Note that the divination takes place undercover, reflecting the *unrevealed* nature of the information being sought. Similarly, the divination rites of Hopi shamans described earlier were conducted undercover. In both cases, the public power of males drew its source from the private power of females. In the case of the Hopis, the female source of power was the as-yet-unrevealed bride who had the potential to bear children (reveal life). The Chandalar Kutchin hunting ritual was conducted by a female shaman after her power to generate life had gone. In hunting, the generative power of females is dangerous. It threatens the power of males to control and kill game. Once the generative power of females is contained (or domesticated), by the production of the food sófki: (as among the Creeks), by the potential to create human children (as among the Hopis), or by menopause (as among the Ainu of northern Japan and Athapaskan hunters of western Canada), it can be used to reinforce and validate the social productivity of males.

The classic anthropological analysis of divination was conducted by E. E. Evans-Pritchard, who studied magic and rituals of the Azande of central Africa. Zande[1] horticulturalists of what is now the southern Sudan traditionally resolved disputes and determined the cause of misfortune by consulting the poison oracle *benge*. *Benge* is a vegetable poison that gains its power to determine human affairs when it is administered to a fowl. The answer is interpreted from the behavior of the fowl when it has ingested the poison and by whether it ultimately lives or dies. According to E. E. Evans-Pritchard, administration of the poison follows a definite process.

The poison used is a red powder manufactured from a forest creeper and mixed with water to a paste. The liquid is squeezed out of the paste into the beaks of small domestic fowls which are compelled to swallow it. Generally violent spasms follow. The doses sometimes prove fatal, but as often the fowls recover. Sometimes they are even unaffected by the poison. From the behavior of fowls under this ordeal, especially by their death or survival, Azande receive answers to the questions they place before the oracle. (1976, 121)

Evans-Pritchard adds, "The poison oracle, *benge*, is by far the most important of the Zande oracles. Zande rely completely on its decisions, which have the force of law when obtained on the orders of a prince" (1976, 121). The poison oracle is likely to be consulted to discover who or what is responsible for any misfortune, to decide on cases of adultery, to find out why a wife has not conceived, to gain information before choosing a new homestead site, or in a host of other contexts in which human experience is not sufficient to determine the course of events.

No important venture is undertaken without authorization of the poison oracle. In important collective undertakings, in all crises of life, in all serious legal disputes, in all matters strongly affecting individual welfare, in short, on all occasions regarded by Azande as dangerous or socially important, the activity is preceded by consultation of the poison oracle. (Evans-Pritchard 1976, 122)

After the poison has been administered to the fowl, the individual who seeks an answer from the oracle addresses his question to the poison. A questioner who wants to know whether a certain man or woman has committed adultery may ask as follows:

Poison oracle, poison oracle, you are in the throat of the fowl. That man his navel joined her navel; they pressed together; he knew her as woman and she knew him as man. She has drawn *badiabe* (a leaf used as a towel) and water to his side (for ablutions after intercourse); poison oracle, kill the fowl. (Evans-Pritchard 1976, 138)

In this case, if the fowl dies, the couple are guilty. The question will be rephrased as poison is administered to subsequent fowls until the verdict is clear to those hearing the case.

Azande are well aware that *benge* is a poison, but they believe that it is activated by the process of rendering a decision with respect to the affairs of human beings. The "power" of the poison does not emanate from "natural laws" but from its place in the divination ritual, the symbolic process involved in making the poison and submitting the question to the oracle. As Evans-Pritchard puts it, "Azande observe the action of the poison oracle as we observe it, but their observations are always subordinated to their beliefs and are incorporated into their beliefs and made to explain them and justify them" (1976, 150).

In studying the poison oracle among the Azande, Evans-Pritchard reports that he behaved toward the oracle and took oracular verdicts as seriously as did the Azande. "I always kept a supply of poison for the use of my household and neighbors and we regulated our affairs in accordance with the oracles' decisions. I may remark that I found this as satisfactory a way of running my home and affairs as any other" (1976, 126).

RITES OF PREPARATION

Though rites of preparation have been widely observed by anthropologists—especially those rites that involve preparation for war—they have not been so systematically studied and analyzed by anthropologists as have some other forms of ritual. This is true even though a number of anthropologists have noted that rites of preparation for warfare may be more elaborate and of greater duration than the act of war itself. This is especially apparent among New Guinea horticulturalists, whose pattern of warfare consists of the raid. Their rituals of preparation may include ceremonial boasting and threats, magical preparation of warriors and weapons, and sexual abstinence. On the other hand, their raids typically last only until someone on the opponent's side has been injured or killed.

Among the Dani of New Guinea, observed by Karl Heider, preparations for battles begin the night before. Every battle is sponsored by a Big Man, a leader who exerts influence over others through his ability to persuade and distribute resources. The Big Man has a claim on any trophies taken during a battle, but he also takes some of the blame if one of his comrades is killed. The evening before a battle, the Big Man holds an *elak gabelhatek*, literally the sharpening of the spears and arrows. The ritual helps to prepare for the coming battle and is aimed at enlisting the aid of ghosts (Heider 1991, 100–101). "The Dani believe that when people die their ghosts remain in the vicinity of their homes and are a potential cause of trouble for the survivors, but in warfare the ghosts can be induced to assist against the enemy" (Heider, 109).

Ghosts help protect a village by raising the alarm if an enemy approaches. They also help kill an enemy in battle: "The ceremony which is held the night before a battle is apparently intended in part to send the ghosts over to the enemy side, where they select out a victim to be killed on the battlefield the next day. There is a feeling that human weapons need this ghostly assistance in order to kill an enemy" (Heider 1991, 109). Note that, among the Dani as among the !Kung, the acts of spirit beings do not displace the acts of human beings. Rather, the acts of spirit beings make possible the acts of human beings.

During the ceremony, food is offered to the ghosts but is actually eaten by humans, as is generally consistent with food offerings to gods and spirit beings cross-culturally. It is believed that the gods or spirit beings consume the essence of the food offered to them but have no need of the food's material manifestation. In Dani rites of preparation for battle, a pig is killed, and a portion of it is offered to the ghosts. Among New Guinea horticulturalists, the number and quality of pigs a man owns marks his status. Pigs are killed only on ceremonial occasions.

Dani Warfare

Early on the morning of the battle, the Big Man sends a messenger to offer a challenge to the opposing side. The challenge is usually accepted by a Big Man on the other side, after which a battlefield is agreed on.

> Then the whole countryside erupts in the cry of the *jokoik*, the large cuckoo dove—literally a war whoop—as word is passed across the entire alliance. It is a clear message. Everyone knows where it originated, so they know that there will be fighting that day on that front. The cries are both announcement and invitation. (Heider 1991, 101)

Men on both sides adorn themselves for battle, arranging feathers in their hair and adjusting their ornaments. "Both men and weapons are smeared with cosmetic pig grease" (Heider 1991, 101). After a couple of hours spent in the warriors' assembling on the battlefield, the battle gets under way, with a few men running toward the enemy, waving their weapons and feather whisks, shouting taunts, and whooping the battle cry. Gradually, the opposing lines get closer together and begin firing off their arrows.

Since the flight of an arrow is highly visible at close range, Heider notes, most people are able to dodge the arrows, though wounds may be inflicted as the men drop back from the line of battle. "For most, a battle is full of excitement. There is a tremendous amount of shouting, whooping, and joking. Most men know the individuals on the other side, and the words which fly back and forth can be quite personal" (Heider 1991, 104). "Connoisseurs on both sides would laugh heartily when a particularly witty line hit home" (104). Heider notes that the battles often end when it begins to rain or the men begin to lose interest and drop out of the fighting.

Mae Enga Warfare

The Mae Enga of Papua New Guinea follow similar preparations for battle. In this group as well, Big Men play an important role in deciding when it is time to go to battle and in conducting preparation rites. Several pigs contributed by important men of the clan are killed and prepared for a feast. The blood and "vital essence" of the pig are formally offered as food to the ghosts of men who have previously been killed by the clan about to be attacked. Anthropologist Mervyn Meggitt describes the meaning of the rite.

> This dedication informs the ghosts that their agnates [kin related through male links] are about to avenge their deaths and exhorts them to restrain their characteristic domestic malevolence and not lead their "brothers" into danger during the combat. At the same time this ritual is thought to propitiate in a general way all the clan ancestors, to impress upon them that their descendants are not afraid to fight and die for the interests of the clan. (1977, 81)

In this ritual, the primacy of the group over the fate of the individual is made explicit.

Mae Enga may engage in "oven-divination," which predicts how the battle is likely to go. Certain insects emerging from the oven mound "foretell success and indicate the number of men the enemy will lose" (Meggitt 1977, 81). Other signs, such as the presence of earthworms in the oven pit or tubers that break while cooking, indicate deaths among their own clansmen (Meggitt, 81). Unless the omens are numerous and uniformly indicate disaster, it is unlikely the battle will be called off, since the Mae Enga consider casualties to be part of warfare. If, however, the "verdict" of oven-divination is disaster, the Big Man and fight leaders may call off the attack.

Unlike the Dani, Mae Enga carry out their attacks amid a great deal of secrecy. The Mae Enga avoid calling on the aid of allies unless absolutely necessary, carry out their attacks just before dawn, when the enemy is likely to be caught off guard, and are wary of mixed allegiances among members of their own clan. Because Mae Enga marry outside their own clan, members may have loyalties to their wife's relatives in another village or to their mother's brother who resides in another village.

> In one case I was told of (and it is presumably not unique), the men of a clan so distrusted a "brother's" attachment to his close kinsmen among the enemy that they not only excluded him from their initial deliberations, but also, once they had decided to fight, kept him under restraint, tied with pig ropes and guarded by the old men, until the attack was launched. (Meggitt 1977, 81)

Though the ritual preparations are similar, the Dani and Mae Enga represent different approaches to warfare. As Heider's description indicates, there is little demarcation among the Dani that distinguishes the ritual preparation from the battle itself. Both involve a degree of formality and mutually agreed upon expectations for appropriate behavior, as well as occasions for social bantering and exchange within and between the groups involved. Dani battles have much the same flavor as sporting events. On the other hand, Mae Enga battles are marked by antagonism, suspicion, and secrecy.

Athletic Rites of Preparation

Rites of preparation used by professional athletes may range from a two-minute prebatting sequence to an elaborate pregame complex. As with the Dani and Mae Enga, rituals of athletes in professional team sports begin the night before the game. Some professional football teams check their players into a hotel the night before a game, even if the game is played at home and there is no technical necessity for lodging the players. Some professional athletes playing for teams that do not follow this custom check themselves into a hotel the night before a game. In some cases, an athlete may share a hotel room with his customary roommate on "away" games.

The night before a game, an athlete may check to make sure the door or window of his bedroom is positioned the same way as before a previously successful game, that his day-of-the-game clothes (which may be "lucky") are ready for him, and that he is sleeping on the "correct" side of the bed, "so that his world is in its proper place for the beginning of the game" (Womack 1982, 238). This careful concern for starting "correctly" on the day of a game helps the athlete both to focus on the game and to realign his social allegiances. "Before a game an athlete must turn his attention from the concerns and social relationships of everyday life and prepare himself to assume the responsibilities and loyalties of sports" (Womack 1982, 238).

Most professional athletes have elaborate day-of-the-game rituals, such as that described by hockey player Dennis Abgrall:

> When you win, you try not to change anything. Nothing. You do everything exactly as you did the whole day of your win. Beginning from the time you get up, was your window/door open? Get up on the same side of the bed. Eat the same meals, at the same places—home or at the same restaurant—nothing extra. If your salad was dry, order it dry again; if you had a large milk, then again; if your steak was ordered medium, then again; no dessert, and so on. You leave at the same times, take the same routes, park in the same place, enter through the same door, and prepare for the finale—game time—with the accent on precision. (Womack 1982)

The athletes' rituals prepare them for the physical and psychological demands of competition. Other members of the team or fans may support the athletes and ease their own anxieties by enacting rituals of their own. Tommy Lasorda, the longtime manager of the Los Angeles Dodgers, confirms that this kind of ritual is common in sports. "If we won the game the night before, I try to do everything the same way. But I don't get to the point of wearing the same clothes, like some do" (Womack 1982).

Since these rituals typically are designed and performed by individuals, sociological explanations for use of rituals do not wholly explain their importance. A more satisfactory explanation is offered by the athletes, who say the rituals get them "psyched up" for the game. "Psyching up" is not simply a matter of achieving maximum excitement. Participating in sports requires concentration as well as the ability to control adrenalin-charged bursts of strength and speed. The player must be fully alert and focused on the game to play at "110 percent."

No athlete can control the outcome of the game; nor can he completely control his performance, since this depends on such factors as his overall state of health and the performance of other players. Preparation rituals allow him to exert control over factors that *are* subject to his manipulation: when, what, and where to eat; what to wear; and more subtly, his relationships with family and teammates, who recognize the importance of winning for their own interests. Athletes respect each other's rituals because they know their value in improving concentration and increasing the likelihood of winning a game. By ritually controlling the day of the game, the player symbolically controls his own performance, his relationships with others, and ultimately, perhaps, the outcome of the game (Womack 1982, 1992).

RITES OF PROTECTION

Once while traveling through Mexico, I hired a car and driver to take me from Cuernavaca to a village in some nearby mountains. The car, when it arrived, was somewhat dilapidated, and I was uneasy about whether we would actually reach our destination. I attributed my uneasiness to having been socialized in the United States, a country where cars are expected to run smoothly and arrive on time. While waiting for my luggage to be loaded into the trunk of the car, I occupied myself with observing the array of religious statues and ornaments that decorated the windshield and dashboard of the car. At the time, I was taken by the contrast with the more ascetic Roman Catholic art of my childhood. As we prepared to leave, the driver made a quick "sign of the cross" before starting the car.

This gave me a new perspective, both on the potential safety of the vehicle and on the ritual use of the "sign of the cross." I had dismissed my own anxiety as ethnocentric, but if the driver, who presumably knew the potential of his car, was also nervous—well! At the same time, I was fascinated by this new use for a ritual I recognized from my childhood. As a child I had often made the "sign of the cross"—touching the fingers of my right hand to my forehead, chest, left shoulder, and right shoulder while saying "In the name of the Father, and the Son, and the Holy Ghost. Amen." But for me and my family, it was a rite of intensification. For my Mexican driver, it was a rite of protection.

Rites of protection differ from other types of rituals in that they are primarily directed toward controlling vague, undefined, or potentially threatening events or situations. Rites of protection often incorporate taboos (ritual avoidance) and fetishes (power objects, people, or places). An example of a taboo in baseball is the practice of avoiding the word "no-hitter" when a no-hit game is in progress. Rogie Vachon, the famed goalie and later manager for the Los Angeles Kings hockey team, would not allow defensemen playing for the team to sit with their hockey sticks crossed before a game. As a goalie, Rogie was a symbol of power for the team. Hockey players frequently tap the goalie's knee pads or the goal before each period of a game. In other words, Rogie was himself a fetish.

Both hockey players and football players have fetishes in the form of "lucky" defensive equipment. In hockey, goalies often have a "lucky" mask. American football players have fetishes associated with their defensive equipment. I was once in the locker room of the Rams football team when they were based in Los Angeles. The players had all gone home after a practice session, and a trainer for the team pointed out that some of the players had left their newly issued protective equipment behind. "They like to keep what worked for them before," the trainer noted.

That defensive equipment should become fetishes is symbolically logical in hockey and football, two physically dangerous sports. Fetishes among tennis players, on the other hand, tend to involve stuffed animals, clothing, and people. Tennis players on the professional circuit often have a "lucky" practice partner. A tennis coach once pointed out the logic of this: The tennis circuit can be lonely and unpredictable. "Lucky" dolls, clothing, and people who care for you can be counted on; nothing else in the life of a professional tennis player can be.

One especially instructive rite of protection was incorporated into the pregame ritual of Dave Hutchinson, a hockey player with the Los Angeles Kings. Hutchinson was a special kind of defenseman called an "enforcer" or "policeman," whose job is to see that players on the opposing team do not unnecessarily "rough up" his teammates. On occasion, an enforcer is sent into the game to "take out" a high-scoring player on the opposing team. Naturally, the enforcer is likely to be involved in fights on a regular basis. Hutchinson had a "lucky" trainer named John Holmes. Before each game, Hutchinson had Holmes tie down the back of his jersey in a special way so that it couldn't be pulled over his head in a fight. That this seemingly technical act was also charged with symbolism is reflected in the way Hutchinson regarded and talked about the ritual sequence. He would not let anyone but Holmes tie down his jersey. In describing his ritual, Hutchinson said proudly, "I haven't lost a fight yet" (Womack 1982).

SYMBOLS OF PURIFICATION

Water, fire, smoke, salt, and various types of alcoholic beverages are metaphorical symbols associated with cleansing or purification because they wash away or burn away impurities. Baptism in the Christian tradition typically involves symbolically bathing the initiate with water. In some cases, the adult initiate is wholly immersed; in other cases, as is the practice with

Roman Catholics, the priest pours holy water—water that has been ritually purified—over an infant's head. The latter case involves both metaphorical and metonymical symbols: the water represents spiritual cleansing, and the small amount poured over the baby's head is a metonymical device for cleansing the entire person.

Ritual purity holds an important place in Japanese life, and ritual bathing is a part of most Shinto festivals. A font of water and a ladle are placed at the entrance to Shinto shrines so that worshippers can rinse their mouths before entering the shrine. The first bath houses in Japan, dating from the seventh century, were a part of Buddhist temples (Buruma 1984, 10).

Sacred spaces are typically purified or cleansed through the use of fire and smoke in the form of candles, sacrificial fires, and incense. Salt is also considered purifying, perhaps because of its historical role in preserving meat. Sumo wrestlers sprinkle purifying salt before every bout. Salt is also placed before Japanese homes. The alcoholic beverage sake is also used as a purifying agent. In many cultures, alcohol is believed to remove impurities, and where they are used sacramentally, alcoholic beverages are symbolically cleansing because they have undergone the process of purification.

Alcoholic beverages typically reflect a dual nature. They are purifying because of their astringent properties, but they also represent growth and abundance. The word *libation*, derived from Latin, literally means "to pour out as an offering." Libation is associated with the idea of sacrifice, which is based on the principle of balanced reciprocity. Humans offer a portion of their food or drink in gratitude to the divinity that made possible their abundance. In the Middle East, dating back to Sumer and documented in the *Gilgamesh Epic*, grapes were associated with the wild state; their transformation into wine was equated with the transformation of humans from the wilderness into a state of culture (see Womack 2003.) In the Mithraic religion, which developed in Persia several thousand years ago, the blood of sacrificial animals was associated with wine as well as with growth or "flowering" and abundance.

Wine and blood are symbolically linked in Middle Eastern tradition. Christ was following in this tradition when he raised his wine glass at the Last Supper and said, "This is my blood; take ye and drink." He was symbolically offering himself as a ritual sacrifice and giving to his followers spiritual abundance. On another level, he was also promising that he would remain with them in the form of bread and wine, the bread representing his body and the wine representing his blood. He translated his human corporeal form into the symbolic corporeal forms of bread and wine.

PARADIGMS, SYMBOLS, MODELS, AND MYTHS

In Western tradition, science and religion are seen as being antithetical to each other. Similarly, the material world is viewed as being in opposition to the spiritual world. This view contrasts with most other worldviews, including the Asian way of thinking, in which the material universe and the spiritual universe are one and the same.

The perceived opposition of matter and spirit characteristic of Western religion and philosophy has a long history dating back to Plato's model of Ideal forms, which are eternal and cannot be perceived by the senses. Plato's account of Socrates' "Parable of the Cave" poses an opposition between the ideal forms of the intellect and the shadow forms perceived by the senses. Socrates viewed these as "higher" and "lower" forms. With the rise of Christianity, the ideal and the sensual became expressed in the opposition between the spiritual and the corporeal. In the writings of the thirteenth-century Christian mystic Meister Eckhart, the opposition between spirit and body is presented as a fierce struggle between "higher" and "lower."

> In you ... the higher faculties should be raised to God, offered up to him and united with him. Indeed, we should assign all suffering wholly to the body, the lower faculties and the senses, whereas the spirit should rise up with all its power and immerse itself freely in its God. But the suffering of the senses and of the lower faculties does not affect the spirit, any more than these temptations do, for the greater and more fierce the struggle, the greater and more praiseworthy is the victory and the honour of victory. The greater the temptation and the more fierce the assault of vice which we are able to overcome, then the more virtue we have and the more pleasing it is to God. (1994, 36)

During the sixteenth and seventeenth centuries, the political power of the Roman Catholic Church threatened to stifle the emergence of an empirically based science. Such scholars as Galileo were persecuted by the Church through the mechanism of the Holy Inquisition. The Western distrust of spirituality stems from the long effort of European intellectuals to free themselves from the domination of the Catholic Church, culminating in the Enlightenment of the eighteenth century.[2] Intellectual traditions that do not have this embattled history do not have a concept that science is antithetical to religion or that spirituality and corporeality are opposing entities.

My Comparative Religion class, taught through UCLA Extension, draws students from a variety of occupations and education levels. This diversity makes teaching challenging as well as intellectually stimulating. During one term, two well-educated professional men spent much of the time dismissing religion as self-delusion and superstition. They rejected the idea that systems of meaning encoded in religion are essential components of human social life. During one lecture I was discussing a Hindu cosmology in which the manifest universe arises from Brahman, an undifferentiated creative source that is neither male nor female because it contains everything within itself.

"There is nothing above and beyond the material world," one of the skeptics asserted.

"I don't think Hindus would disagree with that," I replied. "The primary difference between the Hindu paradigm and the scientific paradigm is that Hindus see the creative energy underlying the universe as conscious, whereas physicists see it as subatomic 'particles' or as mutual attraction."

"There is no such thing as a mind," the man insisted. "All thought can be studied as synapses of the brain."

On a purely technical level, he was correct. The mind would not show up in an autopsy. However, the concept that all phenomena are material is greatly overstating the case. Much of the world inhabited by human beings is conceptual rather than material, even when it is based on experience of the physical world. Samuel Clemens (Mark Twain) illustrated this irony in describing his first flight in an airplane over the equator: "There it was, a silvery line all the way to the horizon." Lewis Carroll expresses a similar ironic theme in his poem "The Hunting of the Snark":

> What's the good of Mercator's North Poles and Equators,
> Tropics, Zones and Meridian Lines?"
> So the Bellman would cry; and the crew would reply,
> "They are merely conventional signs!"

Though meridians, parallels, and the equator are traced on maps and globes, they are not traced on the earth's surface. Yet navigators would literally be lost without these conventional signs. Similarly, we would all be lost without our paradigms, the conceptual models that guide us safely through our social and physical worlds. Love is more than nerve impulses. Family is more than a collection of people related by kin ties. Our neighborhood is more than an array of houses on a given street. "Love," "family," and "neighborhood" are meaningful categories that define our social universe. If I say a neighbor is "like family," I am extending to that person a web of relationship that includes emotions and behaviors. Still, my "real family" would probably never expand their concept of family to include the individual whose relationship to me is defined by proximity, no matter how intricate the web of emotions and behavior that links me to my neighbor.

Emotions and behaviors are as "real" in their own way as people, houses, streets, and synapses are in their distinctive ways. The existence of God can never be proved or disproved by application of scientific principles. Science is based on empiricism, which means it considers phenomena that can potentially be observed and measured. To believers, God is a meaningful category that is not subject to observation or measurement. Religious myths explain our experience as social, physical, and experiential beings through symbols. Science explains the phenomenal universe through models, words, and equations. These are not competing paradigms; they are conceptual models that explain various aspects of the human experience. The linguist Edward Sapir writes, "The mind that is intellectualist through and through is necessarily baffled by religion, and in the attempt to explain it makes little more of it than a blind and chaotic science" (1949, 123).

NOTES

1. Zande is the adjective form; Azande is the noun form.

2. For a concise discussion of the historical roots of the Enlightenment, see Paul Brains, "The Enlightenment," http://www.wsu.edu/~brians/hum_303/enlightenment.html.

5

SYMBOLS AND THE ARTS

If you don't know about God, art is the only thing that can set you free."
The speaker of these words is an unusual art critic, Sister Wendy, a
Carmelite nun in Norfolk, England; author of a book on Vatican art; and
host of a television program on art. Sister Wendy adds, "[Art] satisfies and
challenges the human spirit to accept a deeper reality."

It is not surprising that a person adept in the symbolic traditions of
religion and art would find parallels between the two forms of liberation,
since religion and expressive culture speak the same symbolic language.
Both address multiple levels of the human experience through the language of symbols. Tiv horticulturalists of what is now Nigeria use the word
gba, which means "create," to describe two processes only: God's creation
of the world and the act of carving an object of art in wood (Bohannan
1968, 740). Edward Sapir discerns a different relationship between art and
religion.

> [Religion] has often allied itself with art and science, and art at least
> has gained from the alliance, but in crucial situations religion has al-
> ways shown itself indifferent to both. Religion seeks neither the ob-
> jective enlightenment of science nor the strange equilibrium, the sen-
> suous harmony, of aesthetic experience. It aims at nothing more nor
> less than the impulsive conquest of reality, and it can use science and
> art as little more than stepping stones toward the attainment of its own
> serenity. (1949, 123)

Though the term *art* is often used to refer only to the formal visual arts—
painting, drawing, and so forth—it can also include the performance arts,
such as theater, dance, and music.

ART AND SOCIETY

On a social level, the primary difference between religion and expressive culture is that religion symbolically encodes values and social relationships in a way that reinforces the solidarity of the group. Expressive culture, on the other hand, reinforces the solidarity of the group by ridiculing, exaggerating, critiquing, or challenging values and social relationships. On the surface, it might appear that the work of expressive culture would erode group solidarity. In fact, the opposite is true. Expressive culture acts out unacknowledged conflicts and unexpressed frustrations that would, if no means of expressing them existed, eventually produce irreparable schisms in the social fabric. In this sense, expressive culture provides a vent for social tensions.

Expressive culture also infuses a group with flexibility, which prevents it from becoming overly rigid. Every society must be able to absorb change if it is to survive, and every society incorporates the mechanisms for self-reflection in its various forms of expressive culture. Clowns and other creative people poke fun at the serious work of society so that the "serious work" does not become stultifying. Hopis say the best clowns are those who are most serious in their everyday life.[1]

Robert Brightman (1999) notes that clowns among the northwestern Maidu of the Sierra foothills and Sacramento River Valley were initiated *yeponi*, the highest-ranking members of the Kuksu society, an influential male secret society that, among other things, sponsored seasonal rituals and dances. Clowns were appointed by the society and held office for life. The high social status of the clown contrasted with the socially inappropriate activities of clowning. Clowning relied strongly on physical comedy and acrobatics and on ordinarily culturally inappropriate actions such as stealing food and "dancing like a woman." "The clown acts a deviant role and his transgressions are multiple. Refusing, except under duress, appropriately to perform his ostensible ceremonial roles . . ., the clown instead engages in joking, lying, inappropriate eating, begging, pilfering, and malingering" (Brightman 1999, 276).

Victor Turner uses the terms *structure* and *antistructure* to refer to the relationship between the usual work of society—producing food and other material goods, organizing power relationships, and negotiating kin relationships—and the work of symbolic activities, such as art and festivals. Turner describes "two major 'models' for human interrelatedness" (1969, 96).

The first is of society as a structured, differentiated, and often hierarchical system of politico-legal-economic positions with many types of evaluation, separating men in terms of "more" or "less." The second, which
emerges recognizably in the liminal period [of rites of passage], is of society as an unstructured or rudimentarily structured and relatively undifferentiated *comitatus*, community, or even communion of equal individuals who submit together to the general authority of the ritual
leaders. (1969, 96)

The people and institutions charged with the creative aspects of a society,
its expressive culture, are associated with *communitas* and are on the margins,
or liminal. "Liminal entities are neither here nor there, they are betwixt and
between the positions assigned and arrayed by law, custom, convention, and
ceremonial" (Turner 1969, 95). Religions that emphasize organization and
membership are part of the structure, but religious activities can also be part
of the antistructure. In hierarchical societies, religious mystics and people
engaged in producing expressive culture live in a permanent state of communitas with respect to those engaged in the more ordinary business of society. Turner uses the terms *liminal personae* and *threshold people* to refer to
those people engaged in the business of communitas. Because they are
threshold people operating on the margins of society, they are often viewed
as dangerous.

Though antistructure critiques and challenges social structure, its objective is not to destroy the structure. Instead, antistructure reinforces and
stabilizes society by providing a means of acting out contradictions that
might otherwise destabilize the group.

George Devereux suggests that art can be "a harmless safety valve." He
cites the response of the seventeenth-century French Cardinal Mazarin,
who on hearing that songs were sung against an unpopular new tax said,
"They sing [and therefore] they will pay" (1971, 203). Devereux adds,
"Where the press [or art] is truly influential, it is always quickly made un-
free. The American press and the American artist are free only because they
have either muzzled themselves—or have nothing upsetting to say" (1971,
203–4). Defining art as outside ordinary reality allows it to make statements
that would not ordinarily be permitted. Devereux writes, "In addition to
viewing art as a harmless safety valve, society and the artist alike consider the
artistic utterance as *unrepudiable* in regard to *form*, but *repudiable* as to *content*
(1971, 204; italics in the original).

The case is not so simple as Devereux suggests, however. Art can provide
an impetus for change, as well as preserve the status quo. Social change and

changes in cultural values can be negotiated in the "not-real" world of art before being implemented in the "real" world that includes the political economy and ordinary relationships. Because symbols are the language of art, and therefore address both conscious and unconscious motivations, change may occur sub rosa before rising to the surface of public acknowledgment.

ART AND CULTURE

According to an old baseball story, three of the most senior umpires at an umpire convention stood surveying the antics of the lesser umpires while seeking a suitable topic upon which to expound. The most junior of the three struck a pose and announced, "Baseball. Nuthin' but balls and strikes. I calls 'em as I sees 'em." After a pause, the umpire next in seniority countered, "Baseball. Nuthin' but balls and strikes. *I* calls 'em as they are." The oldest umpire assumed a suitably dignified stance and averred, "Baseball. Nuthin' but balls and strikes, and *they ain't nuthin'* 'til I calls 'em" (Dolgin, Kemnitzer, and Schneider 1977, 20; italics in the original).

This story illustrates the importance of interpretation in defining human behavior. Just as the umpire defines the reality of balls and strikes for players, spectators, and scorekeepers, symbols shape knowledge as it is conveyed from person to person from one generation to the next and as we interpret our experience of reality for ourselves. Similarly, artists may represent the antistructure of society, but their works of art are constrained by cultural norms. The umpire described above may have ultimate authority in determining the difference between balls and strikes, but he is constrained by the cultural conventions of baseball from calling a particular play a goal or a down. Were he to be so bold, his position of authority would quickly be stripped from him. The umpire has authority over the play, but he does not have ultimate authority; ultimate authority is vested in the conventions of baseball.

Devereux suggests that "the dynamic criterion of art is the straining of pure affect against pure discipline" (1971, 194). Affect, or emotion, provides the impetus to art; discipline is culturally constructed. Discipline defines both the artistic expression and its acceptance in the society in which it is produced: "The discipline itself—the rules of the game—is the means whereby society determines whether a given expressive act represents art or something else, and also whether the product in question is good, mediocre, or bad art" (Devereux, 194). The *process* of making art may seem unruly, but the *product* must conform to cultural expectations.

Franz Boas notes that art rests on the aesthetic standards and techniques of an artist trained within a particular cultural convention. "The manufactures of man the world over prove that the ideal forms are based essentially on standards developed by expert technicians. . . . Without a formal basis the will to create something that appeals to the sense of beauty could hardly exist" (1955, 12). Boas adds that art transforms the experience of the observer.

> The emotions may be stimulated not by the form alone, but also by close associations that exist between the form and idea held by the people. . . . When the forms convey a meaning, because they recall past experiences or because they act as symbols, a new element is added to the enjoyment. The form and its meaning combine to elevate the mind above the indifferent emotional state of every-day life. . . . This is no less true of primitive art than of our own. (1955, 12)

Art is not a literal depiction of reality; rather, it is a culturally defined interpretation of human experience. Devereux describes "style" as culturally prescribed distortions. African, Melanesian, and other non-Western artists distorted the human figure, he writes, not for lack of technical expertise, but "intentionally and in accordance with cultural rules governing artistic utterances" (1971, 200). Similarly, Devereux suggests, European medieval artists carved gargoyles reflecting "their nightmare vision of the human body," which was closely related to "their nightmare vision of the universe and of life" (1971, 201).

Though artistic conventions reflect views of the universe characteristic of particular cultures, they do not represent everyday experience. Rather, art represents a potential reality developed in the imagination of the artist and conforming to cultural expectations. Devereux notes that Greek artists who depicted centaurs and medieval Catholic artists who depicted angels would have been astonished had they encountered these mythological beings in everyday life. Gargoyles, centaurs, and angels are conceptual beings that are symbolically brought to life through the artistic medium.

ART AND AESTHETICS

In his poem "Endymion," the nineteenth-century English poet John Keats wrote, "A thing of beauty is a joy forever." But what, exactly, is beauty? In the same century, Margaret Wolfe Hungerford wrote, "Beauty is in the eye of the beholder." She was elegantly paraphrasing a rather more pompous declaration of the eighteenth-century philosopher David Hume, who wrote, "Beauty in things exists in the mind which contemplates them."

The French anthropologist Jacques Maquet addresses exactly this conundrum in his book *The Aesthetic Experience: An Anthropologist Looks at the Visual Arts*, in which he attempts to analyze the relationship between a work of art and the person who contemplates it. Also to be factored into this equation is the individual or community that fashions the work of art. "A first contribution of anthropology is the construction of art within an encompassing reality" (Maquet 1986, 3).

> In an anthropological perspective, art is not reduced to an ideational configuration of forms; it is situated among other systems such as philosophies, religious beliefs, and political doctrines. It is not separated from the societal organizations that support it (academies, art schools, museum and commercial galleries), nor from the institutionalized networks of the total society (government, castes and classes, economic agencies, and private corporations). It is related to the system of production which constitutes the material basis of the society. (Maquet 1986, 3)

Maquet adds, "Art is part of a socially constructed reality. Our first task is to apprehend that part of the reality and to describe it" (1986, 8). Still, Maquet avoids Durkheim's absorption of the human experience into a collective entity. Maquet notes that the individual, shaped by a social context, relates to art on an intensely personal, and even transcendent level: "When we just look at the object as a whole, without analyzing it, and without associating with it memories and projects, thoughts and feelings, gossip and erudition, we, as beholders, pay attention to the visual appearance of the object: what is visible and only what is visible" (1986, 41). Unlike Eastern forms of meditation, whose goal is to transcend limitations of time and circumstances, "The aesthetic experience results from an encounter between a subject, the beholder, and an object whose forms are aesthetically significant" (50).

Maquet considers the importance of contemplation in the aesthetic experience. The observer of art considers a work of art from a perspective that includes mood, context, time of day, contrasting and complementary forms, and, above all, composition.

> Any artifact with aesthetic quality is a tangible symbol standing for the idea of order. This surprising conclusion from our previous analysis is inescapable. If the configuration of forms in any aesthetic object displays an excellent composition, it necessarily symbolizes order as an idea. Any

work revealing a concern for and achieving visual quality is a statement
for order and against chaos. (1986, 131)

The form that order takes is related to the world view of the society in
which it is defined. James Fernandez writes of the Fang, a subgroup of the
Bantu in northwestern equatorial Africa: "What is aesthetically pleasing to
the Fang has . . . a vitality that arises out of a certain relationship of contra-
dictory elements. The Fang not only live easily with contradictions; they
cannot live without them" (1968, 625).

ORDER AND OPPOSITIONS

Oppositions in Fang art are consistent with oppositions in other aspects of
Fang life. The Fang trace kinship affiliation in ascending generations alternately to male and female progenitor and progenitrix. Thus, one lineage
segment is traced to a female founder, next to a male, then to a female, the
whole culminating in a male founder. The system of descent is conceptually linked to attributes viewed as characteristics of males and females generally. Female qualities are unity and common purpose; male qualities are di-
visiveness and conflict. Thus, the female descent group is considered to be
cohesive and fairly stable whereas the male descent group is seen as divisive
and volatile. "The lineage structure systematically distributes maleness and
femaleness so that these two opposing qualities do not clash at the same
level" (Fernandez 1968, 734).

The principle of vitality (life) achieved through opposition and balance is
expressed in the organization of Fang villages, in values attributed to the ideal
human (a balance of female blood and male seminal fluid), and in other aspects
of Fang expressive culture. Fang dances express a balance between male drum-
mers and female dancers, between the low sound of the drum and the high-
pitched voices of women singers, and "the customary scheme by which the
dancers face each other in two opposed lines" (Fernandez 1968, 735).

In sculpture, the Fang aesthetic is acted out in a dynamic tension between the skill of the carver and the expectations of Fang social commen-
tators. "Very often the villagers consider themselves the final cause of the
statue and apply what social pressures they can to the efficient cause, the
carver, to see that the work turns out to their expectations" (Fernandez
1968, 728). Central to Fang art criticism is the issue of balance. The quad-
rants of a statue must be balanced. Shoulders, arms, legs, eyes, and breasts
should not be proportionately different from each other.

Fang would not appreciate, as the Greeks did, a carving of a figure in the act of running, since this would violate the Fang concept of balance. Whereas connoisseurs of Greek statuary would appreciate the gracefulness of the human body in motion, this style of artistic portrayal would offend the Fang aesthetic. Fang would say that, without the balance of opposite members, a figure would not be "a real one" and that "it would have no life or vitality within it" (Fernandez 1968, 730). In terms of aesthetics, this represents a real difference in conventions governing the portrayal and expression of vitality. For Greeks, vitality and "realness" are expressed in the body in motion; for Fang, vitality is expressed in the dynamic tension inherent in balance. "Vitality arises out of complementary opposition and for them what is aesthetically satisfying is the same as what is vitally alive" (735).

VITALITY AND AESTHETICS

For those trained in a Western aesthetic, Greek statuary is valued for depicting the human figure "realistically," whereas Fang statuary would be described as stylized. For the Fang, balance is the measure of realism, and they view their statues as "our traditional photographs." Fernandez explains this type of realism.

> Now I have come to believe after lengthy discussions on this matter— for example, the Fang recognize well enough that the proportions of these statues are not the proportions of living men—that what the statue represents is not necessarily the truth, physically speaking, of a human body but a vital truth about human beings, that they keep opposites in balance. (1968, 731)

Paul Bohannan has similarly noted that art is produced in a social context that reflects a cultural aesthetic. He describes an exchange between a Tiv artist, who was carving a statue of a woman out of wood, and a young man from his compound. By way of greeting, the young man said, "Grandfather, you are carving a woman." When the old man acknowledged this, the following conversation took place.

> "What are those three bumps on her belly?" the youngster asked.
> The old man laid down his adze and eyed the youngster who had interrupted him. "The middle one," he said impatiently, "is her navel."
> The boy was silent for a moment but spoke again just as the old man reached for his adze, "Then what are the other two bumps?"

The old man barely concealed his contempt for questions about so obvious a point. "Those are her breasts."

"Way down there?" the youngster asked.

"They've fallen!" the artist fairly shouted.

"But, grandfather, even if they had fallen, they would not. . . ."

The old man grabbed up his adze. "All right, all right," he muttered, and with three perfectly aimed blows the three bumps came off. (Bo-hannan 1968, 741)

Among the Tiv, figure carvings are almost always made by an individual artist, often guided by input from onlookers. Other aesthetic products—such as decorated stools, walking sticks, and weavings—result from communal activities. An artist may work on an object for a while, then put it aside, where it will be taken up by another. There is no sense of artistic ownership of the product, as in European and North American society. In addition, there appears to be a sense among the Tiv that the artistic product results from a collaboration between the artist and the art object. The design is seen as emerging from the artistic act itself rather than from the control of the artist.

The first time I saw a man sewing raffia almost at random on to a cloth he was preparing for resist dyeing, paying attention to a political discussion rather than to any pattern and obviously having no plan, I was upset. I finally interrupted the business at hand to ask him why he did not pay attention to what he was doing. He told me . . . that one does not look at a pattern until it is finished; then one looks to see if it has come out well. (Bohannan 1968, 743)

Whether an artistic product "comes out well" appears to be beyond the control of the artist, and the evaluation of its aesthetic value is made after the work is completed. In the case of the Tiv weaver, the artist assessed the value of his work in this way: "If this one does not come out well, I will sell it to the Ibo; if it does, I shall keep it. And if it comes out extraordinarily well, I shall give it to my mother-in-law" (Bohannan 1968, 743).

Inevitably, there is a subjective component to the aesthetic experience, such that one's appreciation or lack of appreciation for a work of art may vary with one's mood or the context in which the art is contemplated. Maquet's moving description of his contemplation of Napoleon's tomb, described in chapter 1, illustrates how compelling context can be. On a less elevated level, I once turned in a journalism article to a new editor who had just had an annoying encounter with another writer. When I turned in my article, he launched into a tirade, saying, "Why are you turning in junk like this? You're wasting my time. Edit your stuff before you turn it in."

I went back to my desk and read through the article on which I had worked so hard, intending to change a sentence or two for purely political reasons. As I read through it, I realized it was a well-organized and tightly written piece. Arbitrarily changing it would have disrupted its smooth flow. After considering the diplomacy of resubmitting it without making any changes, I realized that I could change one word without destroying the integrity of the piece. It is a truism among writers that there is no such thing as a synonym. Words have their own rhythm, mood, and texture. No two are precisely the same. For example a "forest" is not the same as a "wooded area." A "lawn" is not the same as a "plot of grass."

I made the substitution of the single word, which slightly altered the mood but did not destroy the flow. Diffidently, I resubmitted the article to the editor.

"This is excellent," he said. "Why didn't you turn it in like this the first time?"

It would have availed nothing had I pointed out that the "excellent" article was essentially the same as the article he had earlier rejected. Any discussion would have centered on a contest over power rather than on a consideration of aesthetic values.

"You're right," I replied. "I should have."

There is an aesthetic of journalistic writing that differs from the aesthetics of other writing styles. Journalistic writing should be spare and devoid of adjectives. Accuracy in reporting is also highly valued. When I switched from journalistic writing to writing books, I found it necessary to adopt a softer writing technique. My perspective also changed from invisible observer to credentialed analyst. Journalist authenticity is conveyed by the sense that the events reported on really happened. As Clifford Geertz notes in *Works and Lives: The Anthropologist as Author*, ethnographic authenticity is conveyed by the sense that the anthropologists has "been there," has actually observed, interacted with, and understood the people he or she describes. Analytical authenticity is conveyed by the sense that the scholar has command of the literature. This is typically addressed by reciting one's theoretical genealogy.

While acknowledging that aesthetic values vary from one context to another, and especially from one society to another, Maquet suggests that in all societies, integrity of composition ultimately defines art. "Beauty, the common-language equivalent of our aesthetic quality, is not only in the eye of the beholder. Beauty is also in the object. In order to offer enough support for the beholder's aesthetic response, the object must have integrity of composition" (1986, 138).

ART, STATUS, AND GENDER

As Bohannan notes in his discussion of Tiv artists, the role of the artist is not an exclusive one in all societies. In societies where there is little differentiation in status—that is, in relatively egalitarian societies—the artistic process is open to all, though certain individuals may be recognized as more skilled than others. In general, however, access to artistic training and production of artistic products is related to one's social position. Some factors identified by Dennison Nash (1968) include one's position in the kinship system, one's status in the group, ascription on the basis of one's presumed ability or personality type, and one's gender.

Among the Kwakiutl of the western coast of what is now Canada, most dances were the province of either males or females. Rights to perform particular dances and to wear the associated mask and costume were inherited. Typically, rights to perform male dances were transmitted from father to son. Alternatively, they might be given by a man to his son-in-law as part of his daughter's dowry. Before performing the dance for the first time, participants were required to undergo a rite of initiation, which typically included abduction of the novice by a guiding spirit (Mitchell 1998, 264; see also Curtis [1915] 1970).

Among the Aztecs of central Mexico, craft production was highly specialized and concentrated in the major urban centers. Artisans specializing in various materials—feathers, gold, silver, precious stones—were organized into guilds and lived in areas of the city dedicated to these specializations. Membership in the guilds was hereditary, and there appears to have been some ranking among the craft specializations. Featherworkers and stoneworkers appear to have been held in especially high regard. Featherworkers in the district of Amantlan, in Tlatelolco, had their own elite school for young men, a privilege ordinarily reserved for children of the nobility (Berdan 1982, 26–27).

Cross-culturally, craft production is specialized according to gender. Among Ainu foragers of northern Japan, only males could carve religious objects out of wood; this activity was strictly taboo for women. Men carved ritual sticks, which had to be offered to the deities on all ritual occasions. Because the sticks were sacred, they could be carved only in the morning, just as all religious activities had to take place in the morning. "During this time, the Goddess of Sun and Moon is in good spirits and therefore able to deliver Ainu messages to other deities" (Ohnuki-Tierney 1974, 35).

Males also carved the five-stringed musical instruments called *tonkori*, because the instruments were viewed as deities. When a tonkori was completed, the maker placed a pebble in the hollow part of the instrument, and the pebble was regarded as its soul. The maker then adorned the instrument by placing colored material and bells around its "neck" (Ohnuki-Tierney 1974, 36). In former times, Ainu did not carve bear figures or use bear skins for trade purposes since the bear was regarded as the most sacred of all deities. The only exception to this was the carving of a small bear head for use in a bear ceremony. The bear heads were passed down through the generations. Early in the twentieth century, Ainu artists began to carve bears for sale to tourists and release bear skins to outsiders.

Ainu women sewed garments from plant materials similar to nettles, from animal skins, and from fish skin. The most prized garment was made from a nettlelike plant in a process that took months to complete. Only elders were allowed to wear this garment, and only elders could wear a garment with red designs. Only women could make or wear a garment made of sealskin, in which white fur from the seal's stomach was artfully arranged with black hair from the seal's back to make the design.

FESTIVALS: COMBINING SYMBOLIC GENRES

Religion and the arts come together in large public festivals. In New Orleans, Mardi Gras festivities developed out of French Roman Catholic observations of Lent. Mardi Gras literally means "fat Tuesday" and refers to the custom of feasting before undertaking the arduous fasting expected during the forty days dating from Ash Wednesday, the beginning of Lent, to Easter Sunday.

Brought to New Orleans by French colonists, Mardi Gras has been celebrated with masked balls and street processions since the seventeenth century. Since then, the festival has taken on characteristics particular to the varied cultures that have shaped the region. Participation in the festivities is organized according to social status, with many components dating from the visit of Grand Duke Alexis Romanoff to New Orleans in 1872. The Romanoff colors of purple, green, and gold were adopted by the city's elite as the official Mardi Gras colors.

The Krewe of Rex was established to organize a parade for the Grand Duke. This krewe continues to dominate Mardi Gras festivities. The King of Rex is also the King of Carnival and presides over a court that includes the Queen of Carnival. Members of the Krewe of Rex are civic leaders, and many are members of the Boston Club, an old-time conservative Christian group. More recently, a number of other krewes have formed. A Krewe of Black Indians stages a parade marked by display of elaborate costumes modeled after traditional Indian attire. There is also a Babylon Krewe, made up of physicians, and a Krewe of Barkus, formed in 1993 and limited to dogs.

HINDU FESTIVALS

Hindus hold a number of important festivals. Among them are two that illustrate the symbolism of the cycle of creation (birth, growth to maturity, and death) as well as cultural differences associated with the various regions of India. Historically, Hinduism is a collection of religions organized around regional deities and religious observations. The word *Hindu* is derived from the Persian word referring to the people living in the region now known as India. The term came to describe the disparate religions of India after the area was colonized by the British.

Two important male deities, Vishnu and Śiva, are worshipped throughout India. Both are syncretic symbols, combining a number of local manifestations. In the case of Vishnu, these are seen as *avataras*, manifestations occurring when Vishnu descends to earth in different guises to restore the world to its rightful course. Śiva's various manifestations are seen as different aspects of his complex character. Manifestations of Vishnu and Śiva are worshipped under different names in various parts of India and typically are associated with myths that recount exploits of the gods in these regions.

Vishnu and Śiva are viewed by scholars of religion as part of the cycle of creation that also includes Brahma. In general, Brahma is conceived of as the Creator, Vishnu as the Sustainer, and Śiva as the Destroyer. Vishnu and Śiva are worshipped throughout India, whereas worship of Brahma is largely confined to northwestern India. The Holi Festival is a celebratory event that centers on worship of Vishnu, especially his Krishna and man-lion avataras, whereas Thaipusam is a festival of penitence centered on worship of a manifestation of Skanda, son of Śiva.

The Holi Festival

The Holi Festival, or Festival of Color, is celebrated in northern India in early spring. On a full-moon night, bonfires are lit on the streets to cleanse the air of evil spirits and symbolize the destruction of the evil Holika, for whom the festival is named. People fill the streets to splash each other with water and throw bits of color into the air. Young men and women break with custom and flirt publicly with each other and, in a symbolic power reversal, wives beat their husbands. Holi celebrates Krishna, a playful manifestation of Vishnu. It is believed that Krishna loved the festival of Holi and celebrated it in the towns of Mathura, Brindavan, Namdgaon, and Barsnar, where he danced with all the girls, especially his favorite, Radha. Thus, the public flirtations of young Indian men and women mirror Krishna's romantic playfulness.

According to legend, Holika was the sister of an ancient demonic king whose son Prahlad was an ardent devotee of Vishnu. The king had become invulnerable through an act of Brahma that protected the king from harm by gods, men, and animals. The king hated Vishnu and tried to punish his son for worshiping the god. The king put his son through a series of trials, including embracing a red-hot pole, jumping off a steep cliff, and being trampled by an elephant. Each time, the boy was saved from harm by chanting the name of Vishnu.

In desperation, the king called on his sister Holika, who could not be burned by fire. Holika made Prahlad sit on her lap and immersed herself in flames, but Holika burned to death and Prahlad was unhurt. The king then challenged the power of Vishnu by demanding to know whether the god was present in a stone pillar in the hall of his castle. As the king struck the pillar, Vishnu emerged from the pillar in his avatar Narasinha (half-man, half-lion) and tore the king to pieces.

Holi is a fertility festival that marks the end of winter and beginning of spring. It also asserts the ascendance of Vishnu over Brahma and validates the importance of the region in Visnaivite belief and practice. The contest reflecting the relative power of the two gods also reflects historical regional rivalries. Mathura and Brindavan are pilgrimage sites for devotees of Krishna, attracting several hundred thousand pilgrims every year.

Thaipusam

The festival of Thaipusam, which takes place in late January or early February, is dedicated to Murugan, a manifestation of Skanda, the son of Siva. Primarily worshiped in southern India, Skanda is a god of war, also variously called Subramaniam, Subramanya, Karttikeya, or in Sri Lanka, Kataragama. The name Thaipusam refers to the Tamil month of Thai. The festival falls on the full-moon day of that month, when the astrological star

Pusam reigns. On this day the goddess Parvathi, a wife of Śiva, gave her son Murugan an invincible lance that would vanquish demons. Thus, Thaipusam commemorates the triumph of good over evil.

Entranced penitents carry a frame decorated with colored papers, tinsel, fresh flowers, and fruit. The frame is attached to their bodies with hooks. Some pierce their cheeks, tongues, or foreheads with skewers that symbolize the invincible lance of Murugan. The lance and the skewers may also be interpreted as phallic symbols. It is significant that this symbol of male power was given to Murugan by his mother. The penitents are supported in their ordeal by wives, husbands, parents, children, and friends.

A SECULAR FESTIVAL

Though festivals originated in religious celebrations, festivals in the United States have become increasingly secularized. In some cases the distinction between sacred and secular becomes blurred. Mardi Gras, described earlier, has become secularized, and many participants are unaware of its religious origins. The Hindu festivals of Holi and Thaipusam are wholly religious, but their spectacular staging attracts tourists as well as devotees. Tourism, in turn, economically benefits the towns and villages where the festivals are held.

The Rose Parade, held on New Year's Day in Pasadena, California, never had religious pretensions. It was instituted by Pasadena's Valley Hunt Club in the late nineteenth century as a way of touting the beauty and climate of the West Coast city. According to the official Pasadena Tournament of Roses website, members of the Valley Hunt Club were immigrants from the East and Midwest who wanted to promote Pasadena. Professor Charles F. Holder stated to an early Hunt Club meeting, "In New York, people are buried in snow. Here our flowers are blooming and our oranges are about to bear. Let's hold a festival to tell the world about our paradise."

The first Rose Parade was held in 1890 and consisted of a parade of flower-covered carriages. The theme of roses blooming on New Year's Day symbolized the mild California weather in contrast to the ice and snow of the East and Midwest. The mildly competitive tone was made explicit when the festival was designated the "Tournament of Roses." It appropriately reflected the competition between the West Coast and other parts of the country, as well as contesting events featured in the festival.

The first festival included foot races, polo matches, and tugs-of-war in the town square. Rose-covered floats were built by sponsoring communities.

In 1902, the first Rose Bowl game was held, pitting the top West Coast football team against the top Midwest team. Perhaps because the Midwest team, Michigan, routed the West Coast team, Stanford, by a score of 49 to 0, the games were canceled and replaced with chariot races, ostrich races, and a race between an elephant and a camel. The more conventional reason given for canceling the football game is that the 1902 football crowds were unruly. In 1916 the West Coast–Midwest American football rivalry in the Rose Bowl was reinstated, and it continued until 1999, when the Rose Bowl opened its fields to national competition.

Whether sacred or secular, whether enacted in flower-covered chariots or on grass-covered fields, festivals enact regional rivalries and reinforce social cohesion within the group. Jack French, a member of the Pasadena Tournament of Roses staff, experienced a strong reaction to his first view of the Rose Bowl stadium. "Seeing that stadium filled, the masses of colors and the spirit and the sounds and the noise and the fan unity . . . I was overwhelmed." French is now the chief executive officer of the group that runs the Rose Bowl. He adds, "I don't even remember the teams, but that feeling renews itself every year. I can't help but swell up with emotion whenever I talk about it. It can bring a tear to my eye."[2]

NOTES

1. From the video *Hopi: Songs of the Fourth World* (Harriman, NY: New Day Films), Pat Ferrero, producer.

2. See http://www.sfo.com/~csuppes/NCAA/Pac10/UCLA/index.htm.

6

SYMBOLS AND SOCIAL CRISIS

Though symbols concretely encode our experience, they are far from static. Because they draw on many levels of experience and are subject to interpretation, symbols can dramatically change both individuals and societies. Consider, for example, the dynamic of religious conversion. An instantaneous burst of insight, a profound encounter with a powerful symbol, can induce individuals to change their way of life or infuse their lives with new meaning. On a societal level, introduction of a new symbolic system or reinterpretation of an existing symbolic system can topple governments and dramatically alter the social fabric. Many revolutions are brought about under the guise of religion.

Symbolically framed revolutions occur during times of social or cultural crisis, when existing institutions or beliefs no longer serve the needs of significant numbers of the population. These revolutions can be triggered by economic crisis, by invasions or warfare, or by other types of social and cultural disequilibrium (see Wallace 1956, 1966, 1969). Social and cultural crises can also trigger other kinds of symbolic coping mechanisms.

SORCERY AND SOCIAL ANTAGONISM

The Fore of the New Guinea Highlands underwent a serious challenge to their worldview and to their social relationships under the onslaught of the disease kuru, which devastated the female population. Between 1957 and 1968, more than 1,100 kuru deaths occurred in a South Fore population of 8,000. Shirley Lindenbaum studied the catastrophe. "Since kuru is predominantly a disease of adult women—the childbearers, pig tenders, and gardeners—its effects on Fore society have been particularly deranging. When the incidence of kuru reached a peak, in the 1960s, the South Fore believed their society was coming to an end" (1979, 6).

In fact, because of the low birth rate due to high female mortality, the Fore population declined precipitously. In 1954, an Australian government patrol officer provided the first official description of kuru:

> Nearing one of the dwellings I observed a small girl sitting down beside a fire. She was shivering violently and her head was jerking spasmodically from side to side. I was told that she was a victim of sorcery and would continue thus, shivering and unable to eat, until death claimed her within a few weeks. (cited in Lindenbaum 1979, 9)

The Fore attributed the cause of disease either to sorcery or to assault by nature spirits. Since sorcery beliefs are an important part of Fore culture and since the Fore have a powerful reputation for sorcery among their neighbors, they believe that kuru is produced by sorcerers in their own society. Lindenbaum writes that in the 1970s, "the Fore reputation for sorcery has become widespread. . . . New Guinea and Australian newspapers carry occasional accounts of sorcery-related deaths in the Okapa region, and in 1973 the government's Law Department inquired into allegations of fifty to sixty sorcery-linked deaths a year at Okapa said to be caused by professional killers who were being paid up to five hundred dollars for murder 'contracts'" (1979, 29).

In 1962 Fore society was in a crisis over the loss of women to "sorcery-induced" kuru. The people began to hold mass meetings known as *kibung* to discuss the emergency, to call for an end to kuru, and to repair the sexual imbalance. Lindenbaum writes: "Reputed sorcerers made public confessions of their past activities, and Big Men [male leaders] appealed to sorcerers still in hiding to come forth and relinquish their evil practices. All other social events came to a halt" (1979, 100).

SORCERY AND MALE PREROGATIVES

Since the Fore believe that men are responsible for sorcery, men bore the brunt of sorcery suspicions. In addition, the traditional organization of Fore society, as well as that of many other New Guinea societies, places men and women in opposition to each other. Access to land is controlled at the level of the lineage, or unilineal descent group, which is geographically centered on a village. Men owe primary loyalty to their lineage and acquire their wives from other villages. Each village represents, de facto, another lineage. Warfare takes place between lineages, and a man may be required to conduct warfare against his wife's village, or in other words, her lineage. Conversely, the division of labor makes men economically dependent on women, who cultivate the gardens and tend the pigs. Gardens are important for subsistence, and pigs enhance a man's status because of their importance in ritual feasting.

In the crisis of kuru, men were the logical culprits since they had both the means (sorcery) and the motives (lineage and gender rivalries). "The sexual selectivity of kuru exacerbated the Fore variant of male-female hostility common in the New Guinea Highlands" (Lindenbaum 1979, 101). In this case, men who killed their own women were also guilty of killing their own lineage since women produced children for the lineage. "Kuru sorcerers plainly had exceeded all bounds, and at the public gatherings they were reproached for this crime against society" (Lindenbaum 1979, 101). At one gathering, a Fore woman chastised the men:

> Why are you men killing off all the women, stealing our feces from the latrines to perform sorcery? We women give birth to you men. Try to find one man who is pregnant now and show him to us. Or go and search the old burial grounds and bring us the skull or bones of one man we women have killed. You won't be able to find any. You men are trying to wipe us out. (Lindenbaum 1979, 101)

The idea of stealing feces or other products of the human body to work sorcery is prevalent in many parts of the world. Hair or nail clippings are used in vodou dolls and in other types of magic. As discussed earlier, this would be called contagious magic according to Frazer's model. It is based on the principle of metonymy. In this case, the feces, hair, or nail clippings continue to have power over the person of whom they were once a part. It is believed that a sorcerer can use these objects to harm the person. Conversely, a shaman can use them to work love magic.

The idea of using cast-off products of the human body to work sorcery or more benign magic is powerful psychologically since an individual so targeted can no longer control these objects, but a sorcerer or shaman potentially can. Thus, sorcery beliefs reflect power relationships and antagonisms within the group.

Fears of sorcery associated with kuru mirrored traditional rivalries between males and females in Fore society. Men had the power of lineage, solidarity, and ritual potency, as expressed in their ability to control sorcery. Women controlled the economic base of male power. Further, their fertility was necessary to perpetuate the male lineage. Under ordinary circumstances, the power of males and the power of females counterbalanced each other, but the delicate balance of power between men and women was toppled in the crisis produced by the slow-acting kuru.

SORCERY AND ACCESS TO RESOURCES

Social and symbolic antagonisms between men and women eventually proved to mirror the biological basis for the kuru epidemic. Kuru was found to be located primarily in the human brain and was spread person-to-person by the Fore practice of cannibalism. The social prominence of males gave them the power to eat pigs, the most desirable source of animal protein, thus avoiding the virus that produced kuru. Women were left to consume less desirable forms of animal protein, such as the dead bodies of humans, thus making them susceptible to the ravages of kuru.

Because the disease was slow acting and there was no immediate and observable relationship between cause and effect, the Fore did not adopt taboos that could have mitigated the spread of the disease. Had the negative effects of cannibalism been more immediate, that cause-and-effect relationship would almost certainly have been reflected in the Fore symbolic system in the form of taboos against consuming the human brain. In the absence of such a feedback system, the power of males overwhelmed the power of women, both in terms of their control over sorcery and their ability to gain their primary source of animal protein from pigs. The result was a threat to the survival of the Fore, biologically, socially, and symbolically.

RELIGIOUS REBELLION

Anthropology owes its current understanding of the role of religion in culture change primarily to Anthony F. C. Wallace, who identified the source and importance of revitalization movements. Noting that religion usually promotes the stability of social groups, Wallace observes that religion can propel a society into dramatic social change in times of crisis.

> Societies are not, after all, forever stable; political revolutions and civil wars tear them apart, culture changes turn them over, invasion and ac-

culturation undermine them. Reformative religious movements often occur in disorganized societies; these new religions, far from being conservative, are often radically destructive of existing institutions, aiming to resolve conflict not by manipulation of the self but by manipulation of the real world. (1966, 30)

Reformative religious movements are known as revitalization movements because they are aimed at "revitalizing" society by sweeping away institutions that have come to be viewed as decadent or corrupt. Wallace suggests that the origins of "all religions and religious productions" may be traced to revitalization movements.

Such a line of thought leads to the view that religious belief and practice always originate in situations of social and cultural stress and are, in fact, an effort on the part of the stress-laden to construct systems of dogma, myth, and ritual which are internally coherent as well as true descriptions of a world system and which thus will serve as guides to efficient action. (1966, 30)

Revitalization movements almost always follow in the wake of colonialism or conquest. Wherever European colonial powers have overrun indigenous groups, revitalization movements in the form of nativistic movements have sprung up. Nativistic movements seek to address the imbalance of power between the colonizer and the colonized.

Europeans did not invent colonialism and aggressive domination of other cultures. Wherever societies are stratified—and this is primarily associated with the food surplus made possible by intensive agriculture—a dominant mode is outward expansion. Early colonial agents were Alexander the Great of Macedonia and Darius the Great of Persia. Whenever the honorific "Great" is attached to a ruler's name, we know it to be a stratified society that expanded its territory through conquest. There are no "Great" men in egalitarian societies, though there often are extremely capable ones.

Through superior firepower and control of the earth's oceans, Europeans were able to subjugate the earth's peoples more completely than had ever before been possible. Overwhelmed technologically, politically, economically, and theologically (through the work of missionaries), indigenous people fought back using the only means left to them: symbols. In many cases, the symbolism was framed in the form of nativistic revitalization movements, religious rebellions against colonizing authorities.

Among the best known of these, from the anthropological standpoint, are the cargo cults of Melanesia. These follow the pattern of millenarian movements, which are centered on the belief that the world is about to end in a terrible cataclysm. After the Armageddon, true believers will be saved by God or some other powerful being. Peter M. Worsley writes, "Thereafter God, the ancestors, or some local culture hero will appear and inaugurate a blissful paradise on earth. Death, old age, illness, and evil will be unknown" (1990, 397). In the case of cargo cults, Worsley writes, "The riches of the white man will accrue to the Melanesians" (1990, 397).

Cargo cults incorporated the symbolism of both the indigenous traditions and the new, introduced religion, Christianity. They also symbolically expressed class inequities introduced by colonialism. Europeans parceled out Melanesian land for their own plantations at the same time they introduced the new religion of Christianity. In coastal regions of New Guinea, "blackbirding"—in which Europeans seized islanders for work on the plantations of Australia and Fiji—had already built up hostility between the native populations and Europeans.

Leaders of cargo cults exhorted their followers to build symbolic landing strips and boat docks to lure airplanes and ocean-going ships, which they believed brought cargo from their ancestors. At the same time, workers refused to labor on European plantations and sought ritual means of returning to the ways of the ancestors. Many cargo cults developed into political movements that later led to independence from the colonizing powers.

SYMBOLS AND ETHNIC "POWER"

Symbolic assertions of group identity in opposition to outsiders do not always take the form of open religious rebellion. As noted in chapter 3, symbols mark group boundaries. Wherever it is necessary for one group or subgroup to live in close association with another, symbols can be a covert means of asserting the status of one's group vis-à-vis outsiders.

Art can provide a means for nonviolent subversion or redefinition of established authority. Kathleen M. Adams (1998) notes that architectural carvings of the Sádan Toraja of highland Sulawesi in Indonesia negotiate relationships between the traditional Toraja nobility and nonnoble Toraja tourist guides; between traditional Toraja culture and concepts introduced by Dutch colonial Christian missionaries and other outsiders; and between Torajas and Indonesian authorities.

A Toraja noble interpreted the motifs of architectural carvings as symbolizing the noble family's roles and responsibilities. "Nobles have responsibilities (such as that of making ritual offerings) both upward toward the deities and downward toward their dependents (peasants and slaves)" (Adams 1998, 332). Younger, nonnoble Toraja tourist guides interpreted the plant and animal motifs on the carvings as representing "Torajas' traditional harmonious relationship with nature" or as "a hope for renewal of the earth's fertility" (Adams 1998, 333). Adams notes that interpretations of younger, nonnoble Toraja tourist guides "speak more directly to the preoccupations of Western tourists" (1998, 333). She adds, "Toraja art is more than a passive ethnic marker. Carved Toraja embellishments are sites for assertion, articulation, and negotiation of a variety of identities and relationships. . . ." When viewed in this light, presentation of Toraja art to tourists and other outsiders "becomes a claim to ethnic group power" that does not necessarily go "hand-in-hand with political dominance" (1998, 346).

Adams asserts that "we can treat Toraja art as a 'weapon of the weak'" (1998, 346), a statement that many anthropologists would agree with. She adds, however, that Toraja art is also a "weak weapon" because "the multivalent quality of artistic emblems of identity that lends them their strength also makes them vulnerable to appropriation by other groups for other purposes" (Adams 1998, 346). This latter statement is more subject to debate, a debate that hinges on often ethnocentric definitions of "weakness" and "strength."

WHAT IS "STRENGTH"?

If one defines "strength" as the ability to seize control of the national political apparatus or to assert one's interpretation of a cultural symbol over that of a competing group, then it is true that the multivocality and polyvalency of symbols may sometimes make them a "weak weapon." If, on the other hand, one defines "strength" as the ability to maintain significant markers of one's cultural integrity, even as national governments rise and fall, then Toraja art is not a "weak weapon." Certainly, Toraja art has proven capable of maintaining Toraja group identity in the face of incursions by Dutch colonial administrators, edicts of Indonesian government officials, and contemporary invasions of tourists. Ironically, those invasions of tourists confer economic power on the Toraja that help them to resist government attempts to erase their ethnic identity.

That different subgroups among the Toraja disagree on what the symbols mean does not invalidate the symbols. Symbols provide material for negotiation. Their polyvalency is their strength. As Gananath Obeyesekere notes, codifying symbols according to some authoritarian code diminishes their effectiveness (1981, 51).

In writing the Public Broadcasting Service television series *Faces of Culture*, I was especially struck by comments of indigenous people who have faced tremendous culture change brought about by European political and economic colonialism, as well as U.S. economic and cultural colonialism. A modern Kwakiutl woman of Alert Bay on the western coast of Canada noted that "many people think we are all gone. . . . But we are still here, and we will always be here." Mayans of southern Mexico believe "they will be here long after we are gone."

THE MUTABILITY OF PUBLIC POWER

Public political power may come and go. Governments may rise and fall. The power of symbols is not dependent on public rhetoric, mass media debate, or the approval of cultural anthropologists. As long as indigenous people maintain their sense of agency and autonomy through dance, architecture, art, or religious iconography, a culture—or a fragment of a culture—continues.

When a government falls, it falls absolutely. Cultural symbols never fall until the last human being in whose very essence of being they strike a responsive chord fades into dust. Secular power fades at the edge of the grave; symbolic power follows us into eternity. The political power of ancient Egyptian pharaohs has long since ceased to exist, but the Egyptian emblem of life, the ankh, helped to fire a U.S. cultural revolution in the 1960s, and the eye of Horus continues to decorate the imagery of North American New Age wisdom seekers. Ultimately, all governments are weak because they are all subject to the vagaries of human experience. Compelling symbols survive the collapse of governments. Which then is stronger?

It is ethnocentric even to compare the power of symbols with the power of government. People socialized into hierarchical governments tend to see the abstract power of government as all powerful. People who do not experience power in hierarchical social institutions can still experience power in the form of emotionally compelling and culturally integrative symbols.

LOSS OF INNOCENCE

Long after ethnic minorities have been economically and politically integrated into the mainstream of their particular societies, they may retain the cultural symbols that mark their unique identity. In the United States, for example, bagels, blintzes, and the Bronx still spell home to Jews even if they neither eat the food nor visit the neighborhood.

Irish Americans have long been fully integrated into North American society, politically, economically, and culturally. Some people of Irish descent have a love-hate relationship with the symbols that identify them in North America: shamrocks, leprechauns, and green beer. "That's all people know of my rich Irish heritage," one politically active Irish American told me. Yet he admitted that once a year on St. Patrick's Day, he dons emblems of shamrocks and leprechauns, wears the color green, and drinks green beer. "What else do I have," he asks, "to say who I am?"

As this Irish American indicates, symbols are important for communicating information about an ethnic group to outsiders. They also help subgroups to define their own identity. This individual knows a great deal about his rich Irish and Irish American heritage—its music, dance, literature, folktales, and contribution to the political, economic, and cultural development of the North American continent. He is familiar with the harsh treatment of nineteenth-century Irish immigrants during the Civil War, in job discrimination, and in jokes that denigrate the Irish. He can sing an Irish-American folksong about the experience of nineteenth-century immigrant Irishmen who fled the potato famine and were enlisted to fight on behalf of the Northern cause in the Civil War as they got off the boat in New York. His frustration with stereotypes about the Irish stems from his belief that the suffering of early Irish immigrants should not be reduced to shamrocks, leprechauns, and green beer.

Symbols associated with a particular subculture can stimulate ethnic pride, signal defiance of assimilation into a dominant culture, and provide a link to cultural traditions that would otherwise be lost. On the east coast of Taiwan, Amis, who are ethnically linked to Australo-Malay peoples, are being rapidly assimilated into the mainstream Chinese culture as a result of repeated migrations to the island by mainland Chinese. Whereas the Chinese are patrilineal, the Amis are matrilineal. Chinese immigrants from the mainland, who now control Taiwan economically and politically, are agriculturalists whose subsistence is organized around rice, whereas the Amis are traditionally yam-and-pig horticulturalists who also exploit a variety of plants and animals, both wild and domesticated. A powerful symbol of the ability of Amis to retain their traditions is their music and dance. Controversy over rights to their music has made the Amis a case study in musical patrimony.

A CULTURAL ENIGMA

In 1993, the German musical group Enigma released a song called "Return to Innocence," which became an international hit and remained on *Billboard Magazine*'s international charts for thirty-two straight weeks. Enigma made millions. The Amis, around whose traditional chants the song was based, earned nothing, and their contribution to the song was not acknowledged. Amis chants provided the inspiration for the hit song, and the voices of a woman and man from the Amis speaking community of Malan in Taiwan were used for the recurring chorus and melody (Anderson 1999, 5).

Though Western artists are aware of the necessity of guarding rights to their own cultural property, they are less attentive to guarding rights to the cultural property of other people, especially those who have been victims of colonial predation. The Amis chants were recorded in Taiwan in the mid-1980s by an ethnomusicologist. The recordings were eventually stored in an archive in Europe, where they were discovered by Enigma. The archive was paid for rights to the music, but none of the money or recognition reached the Amis. The singer Lifvon, whose Chinese name is Guo Ing-Nan, describes his reaction on first hearing the Enigma CD:

> When I first heard my voice on that metal disc, I was so happy. I couldn't imagine that people all around the world could hear my music, the music of the Amis. But then I realized that Enigma had never mentioned my name. He didn't give me any respect. Our tribe doesn't have a written language. All we have are these chants. I just want the world to know that this music comes from us. (cited in Anderson 1999)

The Amis of the east coast of Taiwan are little known outside their own country. Renata Huang, who has dedicated her time to publicizing the musical contribution of the Amis people, provides the following information about their predicament:

> There are [fewer] than 100,000 Amis living today on Taiwan. Since Chinese began to move onto the island some 400 years ago, indigenous cultures have been giving way to the large Chinese population. Most Amis tribal children grow up without learning how to speak their native tongue. Like minority groups the world over, they're obliged to learn the language of the dominant culture. Guo (Lifvon) says this is why he's sparring with the big record company. (cited in Anderson 1999)

Enigma's record company, Capital-EMI, sold the chant to the International Olympic Committee, which used it in advertisements for the Olympic Games. Lifvon has received none of the estimated $40 million made by the productions that grew out of his original chants. He filed suit against EMI and the International Olympic Committee, claiming they had profited from an unlicensed recording without prior consent. The record company fought the suit, claiming that Enigma's production company acquired the recording from a museum collection in France for $3,000. According to Huang, EMI lawyers argued that, since the Amis chant is hundreds of years old and merely performed by Lifvon, he deserves no copyright protection and the music belongs in the public domain.

But these Western legalistic terms of "public domain" do not address the point of cultural autonomy. When the Amis consented to have their chants recorded as part of human cultural history, they did not intend to lose control over the rights to their performance. Perhaps even worse, people hearing "Return to Innocence" are deprived of knowing the people whose evocative music and vivid dance styles provide the basis for the song. EMI has offered compensation to Lifvon, but his lawyer, Huang Sho-lan, says they have missed the point:

> The crux of the dispute lies with Enigma and EMI who failed to respect this man's rights. They think he should be thankful for having his song on their album. But this is wrong. Aborigines might be ignored and looked down upon by many people in this world. But they have rights just like anybody else. It's simple. If you use a person's music, you must respect him. (cited in Anderson 1999)

TECHNOLOGY AS RELIGION

In the mid-1990s I kept students in my introductory cultural anthropology classes awake by proclaiming, "Within the next few years, there will be a new religious movement, and it will draw its religious imagery from science and technology." I later acquired the status of a prophet when the Heaven's Gate cult of San Diego, California, made national headlines.

Members of the Heaven's Gate cult were well-educated professionals, and the group made much of its money from the computer skills of its members. Guided by their leader, members of the cult prepared to board a "space ship" traveling in the wake of the Hale Bopp comet. They believed the space ship would transport them to a better life on another planet.

Bearing "passports" and wearing Nike tennis shoes, members of the cult "boarded" the space ship by committing mass suicide (see Womack 1999).

If the test of a social science discipline is its ability to predict human behavior, symbolic anthropology scored 100 percent on this "exam." The prediction was a relatively simple matter for a symbolic anthropologist. The year 2000 was just around the corner, and millenarian movements have historically developed around the turn of the millennium, a significant marker in the Western calendar. In fact, the term "millenarian movement" is named for events that transpired around the first millennium.

Just before the turn of the first millennium, a number of religious movements developed around the symbolism of the Apocalypse in Jewish and Christian tradition. According to this Apocalyptic vision, God is expected to destroy the world and the ruling powers of evil. Amid the destruction, true believers will be raised to a messianic kingdom organized around and guided by a messiah. At the time of the first millennium in western Europe, the prevailing imagery was related to the second coming of Christ for Christians, during which time Christ was expected to destroy the unbaptised and take true believers to live with him in Paradise.

Most contemporary North Americans are skeptical of the idea of a rescue by a spirit being. In their everyday lives, they look to rescue by the medical or scientific establishment. We don't ask God for a cure for cancer or AIDS. Instead, we ask Congress to allocate funds for research (if we live in the United States). We create babies in a petri dish and implant the embryo in a rented womb. We prolong life, not by prayer, but by measuring caloric and fat intake.

Yet anthropologists know that, when ordinary measures fail, people look for symbols to provide meaning and as sense of order. Cataclysms, social upheavals, cultural crises all stimulate the quest for meaning, but the old gods, heroes, and demons have lost much of their cultural currency. Our contemporary metaphors are medical and scientific.

The form of a millenarian movement remains the same cross-culturally, but the symbols called upon are embedded in one's particular social and cultural context. Where gods and demons no longer strike a responsive chord, the impulses they represent must find another means of expression. A society that has lost faith in the world of spirits must call on the world of science for symbols. We must rely on comets and space ships. In a world where passports are required to travel from one country to another, we must have a "passport" to travel to a world of meaning.

REFERENCES

Adams, Kathleen M. 1998. More than an ethnic marker: Toraja art as identity negotiator. *American Ethnologist* 25(3):327–51.

Anderson, Christian A. 1999. The new Austronesian voyaging: Cultivating Amis folk songs for the international stage. Unpublished ms.

Bachofen, J. J. 1967. *Myth, religion, and mother right: Selected writings of J. J. Bachofen.* Trans. Ralph Manheim. Princeton, NJ: Princeton University Press.

Barth, Fredrik. 1986. *Nomads of south Persia: The Basseri tribe of the Khamseh confederacy.* Prospect Heights, IL: Waveland. (Orig. publ. 1961.)

Bell, Amelia Rector. 1993. Separate people: Speaking of Creek men and women. In *The other fifty percent: Multicultural perspectives on gender relations,* ed. Mari Womack and Judith Marti, 28–35. Prospect Heights, IL: Waveland.

Berdan, Frances F. 1982. *The Aztecs of central Mexico: An imperial society.* Fort Worth: Holt, Rinehart and Winston.

Biersack, Aletta. 1999a. Introduction: From the "new ecology" to the new ecologies. *American Anthropologist* 101(1):5–18.

———. 1999b. The Mount Kare python and his gold: Totemism and ecology in the Papua New Guinea highlands. *American Anthropologist* 101(1):68–87.

Boas, Franz. 1955. *Primitive art.* New York: Dover.

Bohannan, Paul. 1968. Art and critic in an African society. In *Readings in anthropology,* ed. Morton H. Fried, 738–45. 2nd ed., vol. 2. New York: Thomas Y. Crowell.

Bonvillain, Nancy. 1997. *Language, culture, and communication: The meaning of messages.* Upper Saddle River, NJ: Prentice Hall.

Bourdieu, Pierre. 1972. Les Stratégies matrimoniales dans le système de reproduction. *Annales: Économies, sociétés, civilisations* 27:1105–27.

Bowie, Fiona. 2000. *The anthropology of religion.* Oxford: Blackwell.

Brightman, Robert. 1999. Traditions of subversion and the subversion of tradition: Cultural criticism in Maidu clown performances. *American Anthropologist* 100(2):272–87.

Buechler, Hans C., and Judith-Maria Buechler. 1971. *The Bolivian Aymara.* New York: Holt, Rinehart and Winston.

Buruma, Ian. 1984. *Behind the mask*. New York: New American Library.

Cassirer, Ernst. 1946. *Language and myth*. Trans. Susanne K. Langer. New York: Dover.

Certeau, Michel de. 1984. *The practice of everyday life*. Trans. Steven Rendall. Berkeley: University of California Press.

Courlander, Harold. 1971. *The fourth world of the Hopis*. Albuquerque: University of New Mexico Press.

Crain, Mary M. 1993. Poetics and politics in the Ecuadorean Andes: Women's narratives of death and devil possession. In *The other fifty percent: Multicultural perspectives on gender relations*, ed. Mari Womack and Judith Marti, 320–39. Prospect Heights, IL: Waveland.

Curtis, Edward S. 1915. *The North American Indian* 10. Repr., New York: Johnson Reprint Corporation, 1970.

Devereux, George. 1971. Art and mythology: A general theory. In *Art and aesthetics in primitive societies*, ed. Carol F. Jopling, 193–224. New York: E. P. Dutton.

Diehl, Gaston. 1972. *Vasarely*. Trans. Eileen B. Hennessy. New York: Crown.

Dolgin, Janet L., David S. Kemnitzer, and David M. Schneider. 1977. *Symbolic anthropology*. New York: Columbia University Press.

Douglas, Mary. 1966. *Purity and danger*. London: Routledge and Kegan Paul.

Durán, Diego. 1964. *The Aztecs: The history of the Indies of New Spain*. Trans. Doris Heyden and Fernando Horcasitas. New York: Orion. (Orig. written 1581.)

Durkheim, Emile. 1915. *The elementary forms of the religious life*. Trans. Joseph Ward Swain. New York: Free Press.

Eckhart, Meister Johannes. 1994. *Selected writings*. Trans. Oliver Davies. London: Penguin Books.

Elliott, Alan J. A. 1955. *Chinese spirit medium cults in Singapore*. Monographs on social anthropology no. 14 (new series). London: London School of Economics, Department of Anthropology.

Evans-Pritchard, E. E. 1976. *Witchcraft, oracles, and magic among the Azande*. Oxford: Clarendon Press.

Fagan, Brian M. 1997. *In the beginning*. New York: Longman.

Fernandez, James. 1968. Principles of opposition and vitality in Fang aesthetics. In *Readings in anthropology*, ed. Morton H. Fried, 725–37. 2nd ed., vol. 2. New York: Thomas Y. Crowell.

Festinger, Leon, H. W. Riecken, and H. Schachter. 1956. *When prophecy fails*. Minneapolis: University of Minnesota Press.

Firth, Raymond. 1973. *Symbols: Public and private*. Ithaca, NY: Cornell University Press.

Forde, Daryll. 1962. Death and succession: An analysis of Yakö mortuary ritual. In *Essays on the ritual of social relations*, ed. Max Gluckman, 89–123. Manchester, England: Manchester University Press.

Foucault, Michel. 1977. *Discipline and punish*. Trans. A. Sheridon. New York: Pantheon.

Frazer, Sir James Frazer. 1922. *The golden bough*. Abridged. New York: Macmillan.

Freud, Sigmund. 1924. *A general introduction to psychoanalysis*. Trans. Joan Riviere. New York: Pocket Books.

———. 1961. *Civilization and its discontents*. Ed. and trans. James Strachey. New York: W. W. Norton.

Furer-Haimendorf, C. von. 2001. Priests. In *Magic, witchcraft, and religion: An anthropological study of the supernatural*, ed. Arthur C. Lehman and James E. Myers, 97–101. 5th ed. Mountain View, CA: Mayfield.

Geertz, Clifford. 1971. Deep play: Notes on the Balinese cockfight. In *Myth, symbol and culture*, ed. Clifford Geertz, 1–37. New York: W. W. Norton.

———. 1973. *The interpretation of cultures*. New York: Basic Books.

———. 1983. *Local knowledge*. New York: Basic Books.

———. 1988. *Works and lives: The anthropologist as author*. Stanford, CA: Stanford University Press.

Gennep, Arnold van. 1960. *The rites of passage*. Trans. Monika B. Vizedom and Gabrielle L. Caffee. Chicago: University of Chicago Press.

Gilmore, David D. 1993. Men and women in southern Spain: 'Domestic power' revisited. In *The other fifty percent: Multicultural perspectives on gender relations*, ed. Mari Womack and Judith Marti, 185–200. Prospect Heights, IL: Waveland.

Gold, Ann Grodzins. 1993. Power as violence: Hindu images of female fury. In *The other fifty percent: Multicultural perspectives on gender relations*, ed. Mari Womack and Judith Marti, 247–60. Prospect Heights, IL: Waveland.

Goldschmidt, Walter. 1986. *The Sebei: A study in adaptation*. New York: Holt, Rinehart and Winston.

Griaule, Marcel. 1965. *Conversations with Ogotemmêli*. London: Oxford.

Harris, Marvin. 1974. *Cows, pigs, wars and witches: The riddles of culture*. New York: Vintage Books.

———. 1979. *Cultural materialism: The struggle for a science of culture*. New York: Random House.

Hays, H. R. 1958. *From ape to angel: An informal history of social anthropology*. New York: Capricorn.

Heider, Karl. 1991. *Grand Valley Dani: Peaceful warriors*. 2nd ed. Fort Worth: Holt, Rinehart and Winston.

Hertz, Robert. 1973. The pre-eminence of the right hand: A study in religious polarity. In *Right and left: Essays on dual symbolic classification*, ed. Rodney Needham, 3–22. Chicago: Chicago University Press. (Orig. publ. 1909.)

Hixon, Lex. 1992. *Great swan: Meetings with Ramakrishna*. Boston: Shambhala.

———. 1994. *Mother of the universe: Visions of the goddess and Tantric hymns of enlightenment*. Wheaton, IL: Quest Books.

Hultkrantz, Åke. 1987. *Native religions of North America: The power of visions and fertility*. Prospect Heights, IL: Waveland.

Jakobson, Roman. 1941. *Child language, aphasia and general sound laws*. Repr., The Hague: Mouton, 1968.

Jung, Carl. 1956. *Symbols of transformation: Volume five of the collected works.* 2nd ed. Trans. R. F. C. Hull. Bollengen Series XX. Princeton, N. J.: Princeton University Press.

Klima, George J. 1970. *The Barabaig: East African cattle-herders.* New York: Holt, Rinehart and Winston.

Lake-Thom, Bobby. 1997. *Spirits of the earth: A guide to Native American nature symbols, stories, and ceremonies.* New York: Plume.

Lakoff, George. 1987. *Women, fire, and dangerous things: What categories reveal about the mind.* Chicago: University of Chicago Press.

Lakoff, George, and Mark Johnson. 1980. *Metaphors we live by.* Chicago: University of Chicago Press.

Lamphere, Louise. 1974. Strategies, cooperation, and conflict among women in domestic groups. In *Women, culture, and society,* ed. Michelle Zimbalist Rosaldo and Louise Lamphere, 97–112. Stanford, CA: Stanford University Press.

Langer, Susanne K. 1979. *Philosophy in a new key: A study in the symbolism of reason, rite, and art.* Cambridge, MA: Harvard University Press.

Langness, L. L. 1987. *The study of culture.* Rev. ed. Novato, CA: Chandler and Sharp.

Leach, Edmund. 1974. *Claude Lévi-Strauss.* Rev. ed. New York: Viking.

Lévi-Strauss, Claude. 1963a. The effectiveness of symbols. In *Structural anthropology,* Trans. Claire Jacobson, 186–205. New York: Basic Books.

———. 1963b. *Structural anthropology.* Trans. Claire Jacobson. New York: Basic Books.

———. 1964. *The raw and the cooked.* Trans. John and Doreen Weightman. New York: Harper and Row.

Lindenbaum, Shirley. 1979. *Kuru sorcery.* Mountain View, CA: Mayfield.

Lynes, Russell. 1980. *The tastemakers: The shaping of American popular taste.* New York: Dover. (Orig. publ. 1949.)

Malinowski, Bronislaw. 1927. *Coral gardens and their magic.* London: Routledge and Kegan Paul.

———. 1954. *Magic, science and religion and other essays.* Garden City, NY: Doubleday Anchor.

Maquet, Jacques. 1986. *The aesthetic experience: An anthropologist looks at the visual arts.* New Haven and London: Yale University Press.

Mauss, Marcel. 1967. *The gift: Forms and functions of exchange in archaic societies.* Trans. Ian Cunnison. New York: W. W. Norton.

McDowell, Nancy A. 2001. Mundugumor: Sex and temperament revisited. In *Being human: An introduction to cultural anthropology,* ed. Mari Womack, 312–320. Upper Saddle River, NJ: Prentice Hall.

Meggitt, Mervyn. 1977. *Blood is their argument: Warfare among the Mae Enga tribesmen of the New Guinea highlands.* Mountain View, CA: Mayfield.

Mitchell, Donald. 1998. Nimpkish: Complex foragers of North America. In *Being human: An introduction to cultural anthropology,* ed. Mari Womack, 256–66. Upper Saddle River, NJ: Prentice Hall.

Moore, Sally F., and Barbara G. Myerhoff. 1977. *Secular ritual.* Amsterdam: Van Gorcum.

Nash, Dennison. 1968. The role of the composer. In *Readings in anthropology*, ed. Morton H. Fried, 746–78. 2nd ed., vol. 2. New York: Thomas Y. Crowell.

Needham, Rodney. 1972. *Belief, language and experience*. Chicago: University of Chicago Press.

Newman, Philip L. 1965. *Knowing the Gururumba*. New York: Holt, Rinehart and Winston.

Obeyesekere, Gananath. 1981. *Medusa's hair: An essay on personal symbols and religious experience*. Chicago: University of Chicago Press.

Ohnuki-Tierney, Emiko. 1974. *The Ainu of the northwest coast of southern Sakhilin*. New York: Holt, Rinehart and Winston.

Parsons, Talcott. 1963. On the concept of influence. *Public Opinion Quarterly* 27:36–62.

Penniman, T. K. 1965. *A hundred years of anthropology*. New York: William Morrow.

Price-Williams, Douglass. 1999. In search of mythopoetic thought. *Ethos* 27(1):25–32.

Rappaport, Roy. 1968. *Pigs for the ancestors: Ritual in the ecology of a New Guinea people*. New Haven: Yale University Press.

Roberts, John, and Brian Sutton-Smith. 1966. Cross-cultural correlates of games of chance. *Behavior Science Notes* 3:131–44.

Rosaldo, Renato. 1989. Introduction: Grief and a headhunter's rage. In *Culture and truth: The remaking of social analysis*, 1–21. Boston: Beacon Press.

Rosenblatt, Paul C., R. Patricia Walsh, and Douglas A. Jackson. 1976. *Grief and mourning in cross-cultural perspective*. New Haven, CT: Human Relations Area Files Press.

Rumi. 1987. *We are three*. Trans. Coleman Barks. Athens, GA: Coleman Barks.

Sapir, Edward. 1934. "Symbols." *Encyclopedia of the social sciences, XIV*. New York: Macmillan.

———. 1949. *Culture, language, and personality*. Berkeley, CA: University of California Press.

Shostak, Marjorie. 1981. *Nisa: The life and words of a !Kung woman*. New York: Vintage Books.

Skinner, B. F. 2002. *Beyond freedom and dignity*. Indianapolis: Hackett Publ. (Orig. publ. 1971.)

Stein, Philip L., and Bruce M. Rowe. 2000. *Physical anthropology*. Boston: McGraw Hill.

Stocking, George W., Jr. 1968. *Race, culture, and evolution: Essays in the history of anthropology*. New York: Free Press.

Swanson, Guy E. 1966. *The birth of the gods*. Ann Arbor: University of Michigan Press.

Turner, Victor. 1967. *Forest of symbols*. Ithaca, NY: Cornell University Press.

———. 1969. *The ritual process: Structure and anti-structure*. Ithaca, NY: Cornell University Press.

Tylor, E. B. 1871. *Primitive culture*. London: Murray.

Vanstone, James W. 1974. *Athapaskan adaptations: Hunters and fishermen of the subarctic forests.* Chicago: Aldine.

Wallace, Anthony F. C. 1956. Revitalization movements. *American Anthropologist* 58:264–81.

———. 1966. *Religion: An anthropological view.* New York: Random House.

———. 1969. *The death and rebirth of the Seneca.* New York: Vintage Books.

Weber, Max. 1947. *The theory of social and economic organization.* Trans. A. M. Henderson and Talcott Parsons. New York: Oxford University Press.

———. 1958. *The Protestant ethic and the spirit of capitalism.* Trans. Talcott Parsons. New York: Charles Scribner's Sons. (Orig. publ. 1904–05.)

———. 1973. *The sociology of religion.* Trans. Ephraim Fischoff. Boston: Beacon Press. (Orig. publ. 1922.)

Weiner, Annette. 1988. *The Trobrianders of Papua New Guinea.* New York: Holt, Rinehart and Winston.

Wilmsen, Edwin N. 2001. Kalahari subsistence foraging. In *Being human: An introduction to cultural anthropology,* ed. Mari Womack, 263–8. Upper Saddle River, NJ: Prentice Hall.

Wolf, Margery. 1974. Chinese women: Old skills in a new context. In *Women, culture, and society,* ed. Michelle Zimbalist Rosaldo and Louise Lamphere, 157–72. Stanford, CA: Stanford University Press.

Womack, Mari. 1977. *". . . His truth shall endureth unto all generations": A study of the transfer of leadership in Eternal Truth Church, a spiritualist church in southeast Los Angeles.* UCLA master's thesis.

———. 1978. The search for enlightenment in Gardena, California. In *Urban diversity,* ed. James Loucky. Los Angeles: UCLA.

———. 1982. *Sports magic: Symbolic manipulation among professional athletes.* Ph.D. dissertation, University of California, Los Angeles.

———. 1992. Why athletes need ritual: A study of magic among professional athletes. In *Sport and religion,* ed. Shirl J. Hoffman, 191–202. Champaign, IL: Human Kinetics Books.

———. 1998. *Being human: An introduction to cultural anthropology.* Upper Saddle River, NJ: Prentice Hall.

———. 1999. Chasing the comet: Technology as a symbol for the year 2000. Paper presented at the 98th annual meeting of the American Anthropological Assn., Chicago, IL.

———. 2003. *Sport as symbol: Images of the athlete in art, literature and song.* Jefferson, NC: MacFarland.

Worsley, Peter M. 1990. Cargo cults. In *Conformity and conflict,* ed. James P. Spradley and David W. McCurdy, 396–403. 7th ed. Glenview, IL: Scott, Foresman/Little, Brown.

INDEX

ABOUT THE AUTHOR

Mari Womack is a writer and anthropologist specializing in symbols, religion, gender, and American popular culture. She has a Ph.D. in cultural anthropology from UCLA and teaches anthropology at UCLA Extension and Santa Monica College. She is author of three books: *Sport as Symbol: Images of the Athlete in Art, Literature, and Song*; *Faces of Culture*; and *Being Human: An Introduction to Cultural Anthropology*. She is the coeditor of *The Other Fifty Percent: Multicultural Perspectives on Gender Relations*.

Dr. Womack has been quoted in the *New York Times, Los Angeles Times*, and the *Wall Street Journal* and has appeared on a number of television programs, including the *Today* show, applying anthropological insights to contemporary issues. She is currently working on a medical anthropology text called *Medical Anthropology: Models of Health and Healing*.